D0291506

When You Are Facing Change

Resources for Living

Andrew D. Lester
General Editor

When You
Are Facing Change

J. Bill Ratliff

Westminster/John Knox Press
Louisville, Kentucky

© 1989 J. Bill Ratliff

All rights reserved—no part of this book may be reproduced in any form without permission in writing from the publisher, except by a reviewer who wishes to quote brief passages in connection with a review in magazine or newspaper.

Unless otherwise identified, scripture quotations are from The New Jerusalem Bible, copyright © 1985 by Darton, Longman & Todd, Ltd. and Doubleday, a division of Bantam, Doubleday, Dell Publishing Group, Inc. Reprinted by permission of the publishers.

Scripture quotations marked RSV are from the Revised Standard Version of the Bible, copyrighted 1946, 1952, © 1971, 1973 by the Division of Christian Education of the National Council of the Churches of Christ in the U.S.A., and are used by permission.

Book design by Gene Harris

First edition

Published by Westminster/John Knox Press
Louisville, Kentucky

PRINTED IN THE UNITED STATES OF AMERICA

9 8 7 6 5 4 3 2 1

Library of Congress Cataloging-in-Publication Data

Ratliff, J. Bill (John Bill), 1939–
    When you are facing change / J. Bill Ratliff. — 1st ed.
        p.   cm. — (Resources for living series)
    Bibliography: p.
    ISBN 0-664-25048-3

    1. Spiritual life—Quaker authors. 2. Change—Religious aspects—
Christianity. I. Title. II. Series.
BV4501.2.R34 1989
248.4—dc20   89-31960
                                                                              CIP

To

Virginia DeVilbiss Ratliff

and

Betsy Ann and Greta Leigh

who faithfully stood beside me

in my recent transitions

Contents

Acknowledgments

I am indebted to both institutions and persons for support in the writing of this book. Here at Earlham School of Religion, to which I came as part of a major transition a few years ago, I am grateful for the support of faculty and students, as well as for official institutional support. This spiritually rich academic community has provided a context for reflection on the changes in my life and a stimulus for growth.

At Earlham School of Religion, Sarah Forth, Bryan Harness, John Miller, and Phyllis Wetherell met with me on two occasions, to discuss rough drafts. Their sensitivity to the deeper issues and to my feelings for this "baby struggling to be born" was especially supportive in the early stages. Jenneke Barton, in addition to being part of this group, gave generously of her time and expertise in editing throughout the entire process. Carol Tyx and Becky Brumbaugh also read one draft and provided helpful feedback. Tom Mullen, Dean of Earlham School of Religion, encouraged me to consider writing, read parts of the manuscript, and invited me to his class on writing to discuss the process of rewriting and editing.

Over the years Wayne Oates and Howard Clinebell have also gently encouraged me to write and, when asked, have given me specific suggestions. Andrew Lester, the editor of this series, was a great help from the beginning, providing clear yet sensitive feedback, and he faithfully stayed in touch throughout the process.

My daughters, Betsy and Greta, gave me many opportunities to experience transitions as they grew into adulthood. Both of them read the manuscript and made helpful comments. My wife, Virginia, has provided unfailing support and care during the many transitions of our life together, has been especially understanding about the long hours and weekends of writing this book, and has given feedback on several drafts of different chapters. My family has been supportive during the struggles of my recent transitions, so the book is dedicated to them.

To the many persons who have shared their problems and their lives with me in pastoral counseling, I am grateful and awed by their trust. In the case studies and illustrations in the book, names and identifying data have been changed to ensure anonymity.

To all these persons, plus any others whom I may have left out, I stand in gratitude. While the work of writing is intensely solitary, at the same time it is communal. Each person who read the manuscript contributed a unique and helpful perspective.

J.B.R.

When You Are Facing Change

1

Invitation to the Journey

The journey from the head to the heart, as we all know, is the longest distance we will ever cover.... Day by day and month by month we are given the inner and outer experiences that contain God's address to us.

—Elizabeth O'Connor[1]

Our bodies remind us we are aging. Our children grow up. We get a new job or move to another place, or perhaps both. Family, friends, and acquaintances die. We start projects and end relationships. We change our diet or decide to act in a different way. Change is our constant companion.

Change can be managed in an infinite variety of ways. Medical doctors help us deal with negative changes that happen to our bodies, while ministers and churches help with spiritual changes. We go to school to make positive changes in our education or in our ability to be employed. We buy new clothes or get a different haircut or lose weight in order to change our physical appearance.

Change is alternately welcomed and resisted. We like change and sometimes even look for it or make it happen because we are bored or need a challenge. The right kind of change at the right time energizes us. We can put lots of energy into learning something new if we are excited about it. A new responsibility in our faith community—persons of a common religious persuasion who meet together—can capture our imagination and our talents, so that we accomplish a great deal.

On the other hand, change is often resisted. Too much change scares us or overwhelms us. We cannot always know what the result will be when we begin to change. Changes in our past may have turned out badly, and we do not believe this one will be any different. We may be dealing with changes in other areas of our life, so that we do not have the time or energy to devote to another one.

Change produces stress. Even good changes that we want and like produce stress. Stress is our internal response to change and is, therefore, unique to each individual. What causes one person stress will pose no problem to another. An optimum amount of stress is useful because it motivates us to do well. However, too much stress affects our bodies, our relationships, our spiritual vitality, our work performance, and our mental alertness. Too much stress over an extended period of time can result in burnout on the job, physical breakdown, spiritual emptiness, and a deterioration of relationships.

Religious Faith During Change

Change and its accompanying stress force us to turn to our religious faith, if we are open to matters of the Spirit. In our personal lives we want our deepest faith to be a source of comfort and guidance during periods of change and upset. We may discover that our faith is not deep enough to handle a particular change, and in fact our faith is challenged to change as well! Or we may discover that God seems absent to us precisely when we need God the most, which compounds our difficulty.

Support is something our community of faith may or may not provide while we are dealing with significant change. Again, some persons find that when they are hurting the most, the community knows the least how to help them. Anxiety or lack of expertise may cause the community to pull back. At times, of course, the community hangs in there with us through seemingly impossible times, and love becomes incarnate in concrete acts.

Spiritual Questions. At the deepest level, we ask ourselves, "Where is God in all the changes in my life and in the world around me? Is there any order to events? Where do I fit in the scheme of things? What is the meaning of change?" And, above all, "What is God's call to me, at this time in my life?" While our religious faith is implicit in every life experience, we more often turn to our faith during times of trial and upset. The word "religion" comes from a Latin word which means to bind together. When the binding to our lives is coming loose, we are pushed to our fundamental religious roots. When life around us appears shaky and unstable, we want to find a rock on which to stand. Our faith in God may provide such a rock.

Spiritual Convictions. God creates, sustains, guides, and renews us; that is my fundamental conviction. The solace that faith provides in times of change is grounded in this conviction. God calls us into personhood through parents and other loving, challenging persons. As we grow, God calls each of us to be co-creators in the continuing work of creation in the world. Each of us has a call from God to join in that partnership. Each of us has some splendid work to do as co-creators of God's realm. It is a splendid work, not because it is widely recognized or heroic but because it is given to us by God.

I believe that, as one writer puts it, "A human being is a longing for God and nothing else than God will satisfy us."[2] That longing may burst forth into consciousness more forcefully during a time of transition. We may become more aware of what we have been missing in our life and what we yearn for the most. We realize that we have been living on the surface and denying our longing for God.

Change is an organic part of the creation. To have a beginning and an end as a created being means that change is built into the created order. All of creation is good, as Genesis 1:31 reminds us. This means that change can be used as a way to grow and to deepen. "We are well aware that God works with those who love [God], those who have been called in accordance with [God's] purpose, and turns everything to their good" (Rom. 8:28). My faith stance is that in some way God is providing *for me* through this change; therefore I need not fear it. I can be open to it, learn from it, and listen to what God is saying to me in the experience.

God is present in the circumstances of our lives. If we are open, God will guide us, even as God calls us out of safe places into new territory. I will talk more about the call of God in chapter 3.

Transitions

A transition occurs when we enter into a time of personal change where we are passing from one condition or state to another. This book is written for persons who have been, are, or will be going through important personal transitions. Its purpose is to provide a perspective from which we can view the transitions that occur in our own lives and in the lives of others. Insights from the Bible, theology, and ethics will provide a Christian perspective. Information from psychology, sociology, biology, and the helping professions will be integrated with and expressed from within this basically Christian perspective.

I have found in my work as a pastoral counselor with people in transition that feelings of confusion, anxiety, and wanting to flee are *normal* at a particular stage in any important change. I have experienced such feelings during times of transition in my own life. In this book, I will encourage you to pay attention to each stage of your transition and its accompanying feelings and needs. I will provide resources which can help as you cope with transitions. Furthermore, I want to look at the process of change from the context of your religious faith.

Personal transitions are a crisis for us. The Chinese word for crisis includes two characters—one that means danger and one that means opportunity. A transition has both possibilities for us. In a transition we can experience disintegration or growth. I hope to show in this book that the way we deal with our transitions makes growth possible.

Transformation from Transition. Transition can be an avenue of spiritual growth, of revelation from God, and even of *transformation*. I am convinced that it is possible to deal with the transitions in our lives in such a way that the changes will be not only good but *transformational.* If we listen for the voice of God, we can emerge from a time of major change more whole than when we entered.

Judith obtained her degree from graduate school. She and her husband, Bruce, moved to another city where Judith had been offered a college teaching position. Bruce had been happy in his former home and job, and had difficulty making the adjustment to a new location. In pastoral counseling, they discovered that a number of issues were sapping the health of their marriage: Judith's history of giving in to what Bruce wanted, and Bruce's feeling threatened in giving in to her this time; Judith's way of making and communicating the decision to move without hearing Bruce's feelings, and Bruce's general difficulty with communicating his feelings. After working on their relationship, Judith and Bruce found that they were able to talk for the first time about some of these issues. Judith became more aware of the way her behavior was affecting Bruce, while Bruce became better able to express his feelings and desires. As a result of this painful experience, their relationship grew and deepened. With the new openness in communication, both found that they liked their marriage even better. In looking back, they acknowledged that their marriage had been rather bland because some important dimensions to their relationship were being ignored. The crisis of the move helped them raise these problems to the surface and deal with them. The result was a more fulfilling relationship than they had yet experienced.

God calls us into new places. As we heed that call, we experience renewed energy and vision for understanding who we are and pursuing what we are doing. God provides the resources and gifts along with the call. As we respond to the call, we will be transformed. I have experienced that for myself and have seen it occur in others. Consider the case of Juanita.

Juanita was a mother devoted to her husband and her three children. She enjoyed her children and felt a strong duty to be home while they were growing up. After the youngest child graduated from high school, the role she had filled for over twenty years was no longer needed. She felt at loose ends and wondered what to do with herself. Her volunteer work did not fill the void. After talking with her husband and friends, she decided to finish the college work that she had dropped when she married. She discovered that she enjoyed studying and learning new things. She went on to graduate school and later became a therapist on the children's unit at the local community mental health center. Her joy and experience in being a mother were transformed into a satisfying vocation.

The experiences of Bruce and Judith with their marriage and Juanita with her career are good examples of the positive benefits that can come from transitions. There was a lot of hard work in both cases; brief descriptions do not adequately convey the nuances and complexities of the situations, and the outcomes were not perfect in either case. However, Bruce and Judith's marriage was happier, and Juanita found her life more fulfilling. The work of going through the transition was worth it.

Transitions are not easy, but the rewards can be surprisingly satisfying. We can learn how to live through our transitions so that growth and transformation are possible. Join me, then, for the journey into ways to do them well.

Description of the Book

In the following pages, we will look at the different dynamics of transitions, including the following questions: Is the transition a result of our own decision? Is the change desirable? Will it take a long time? Are we the only one experiencing the transition? How predictable is it? In major transitions, and sometimes even in small ones, we have a great deal at stake: our security, our identity, and our belief system about the world and about God. The result can be a great deal of anxiety. However, in the midst of the change we possess resources and develop strategies with which to cope.

We will look at the three phases involved in any important transition—an ending, a "wilderness" time, and a new beginning. Each chapter will be organized in the same way: The characteristics of the particular phase of transition will be examined, the feelings and issues that may arise will be discussed, a variety of ways of responding to that particular phase will be proposed, and some suggestions for help along the way will be provided. When we look in detail at each phase, we will find that paying attention to what is going on inside ourselves, and to what God is calling us for, will help us make creative use of the transition.

The word "phase" is used to describe parts of the transition, rather than "stage" or "step," because the process is not always linear from one period to the next. There is some overlapping, a circling back to pick up loose ends, and sometimes a redoing of an earlier period. "Phase" seems to be most apt in describing the different parts of the process that we go through during a time of transition.

Throughout the book we will look at the family and the community of faith as the two important contexts in which we live and which aid or hinder our moving through the phases of our transitions.

How to Use This Book

The persons most likely to benefit from reading and living with this material are those who have lived through some major transition and are curious about learning how to do it differently or more smoothly next time, those who are currently in a time of personal change and are able to think clearly and reflect on their experience, and those who help others to traverse the uncertain ground of change. The end of each chapter will contain some suggestions for personal reflection. Spending time and focused attention on the suggestions will help you to personalize the material and begin to use what has been discussed.

If you are in the middle of a major transition, you will have to discover your own way to make the best use of this book. A particular chapter may fit you more than others, so you may want to focus your initial reading there. Chapters 3, 4, and 5 on the phases of transitions may be most practical and immediately helpful. Working on the sections for personal reflection may require too much energy right now, and that is okay. Give yourself permission to do it your way. Some people who are in the middle of chaos do not read, while others read voraciously. Some people need practical suggestions, not more information, and may want to turn to the section in each of these chapters that deals with helps along the way.

If you are struggling to survive, you may need to put this book aside until you have more inner space and energy with which to work with the material. Reading it after the worst of the crisis is over may help you to learn from the transition and be better prepared for the future. Learning from personal suffering is one way to redeem it. Rereading the book as you go through different stages of a major transition might be helpful.

The book may be used in a small-group setting. One chapter could be read before each meeting. The suggestions for reflection could then serve as the focus for group discussion and dialogue.

For Personal Reflection

At what points does this chapter strike a chord within you?

Recall some of the important changes you have gone through. What changes are you going through right now?

What would you like to learn about transitions and the way you handle change?

What additional ways of coping would you like to have available for use?

What do you hope to get from reading this book?

2

The Dimensions
of Transitions

"Who are you?" said the Caterpillar. . . .
Alice replied, rather shyly, "I—I hardly know, Sir, just at
present—at least I know who I was when I got up this morning,
but I think I must have been changed several times since then."
— **Lewis Carroll**[1]

The outcome of any transition is the result of an interaction among the following areas: the characteristics of the particular transition, the coping abilities and liabilities of the particular individual, and the context.[2] This chapter will look at the nature of the particular transition, while the following chapters will deal with the individual and the context as it affects the individual.

Common Aspects of Transitions

While transitions come in all sizes and shapes, there are various aspects of all transitions that may help us understand them. This chapter will discuss the differences which these aspects make in our response to change. We can then be in a position to understand better our responses to change. Each aspect is listed below as the option between two extreme positions. In reality each aspect involves a continuum between the two extremes and should be understood that way. At any particular moment during a transition, we are located somewhere along the continuum for each of the following aspects.

Control–Lack of Control. All of us need to have a certain amount of control over our lives, if we are to feel secure and good about ourselves and the world. The amount of control we seem to possess, both at the beginning and during a transition, is important in the way we deal with it. Whether or not the change is something we initiated makes a big difference. Although the actual decision may be hard, a job change that we have chosen is likely to be easier to handle than one that is forced upon us. Adjusting to a move across country is different when we remember that we chose to move. A close friendship that becomes a more casual relationship is easier to deal with if we feel that we had some say in the matter.

The difficult part in *voluntary* transitions can be the fact that we cannot blame anyone else if the outcome is negative. We may have been in control of making the initial decision, which led to consequences we did not foresee and over which we have *no* control. We have to take responsibility for our choice and wonder whether we made the right one.

We can fool ourselves in this area. What appears to have happened *to* us on the surface may, on closer examination, really be something in which we had a hand. When looking at why we were fired, it might become obvious that there were times we were intentionally late for work or stayed home to avoid a task or a person. It is possible that we did not like the job and were not suited for the position, so, rather than leaving, we managed to have someone else make the decision for us to leave. When it is hard to take responsibility for a decision, it is tempting to get someone else to take responsibility for us. The change then appears involuntary; we can be angry at what happened to us, rather than taking charge of the change or learning from it.

The other side may also be true. In our psychologically oriented age, we may assume personal responsibility for a lot more things than we rightfully should. Instead of being our fault, for example, losing a job may be the result of office politics, the personality of our supervisor, or the financial health of the company. With the recent trend in our culture to confront people with the importance of taking more responsibility for their own physical health, we may feel getting sick is our fault when it really is not.

If we do not take the responsibility, we put it somewhere else. It is our boss's fault, or the company's, or God's. As Rabbi Harold Kushner has shown in *Why Bad Things Happen to Good People*, [3] we have such a need to believe that someone is in control of events that we blame God for bad things. Unexplained chaos creates anxiety.

The truth probably lies somewhere in the middle. Most changes have aspects that are in our control and others that are not. The more control we feel in a situation, the easier it is to adjust to the change. Hospitals have found, for example, that patients who need pain medication use less of it and feel better when *they* are able to decide when to release medication into the IV tube. We still may have difficulty with the change, but it helps to know that in some sense we chose it and have some power to make the adjustments and influence the outcome.

In changes we brought on through our own decisions, we may feel that we *had* to choose the way we did in order to avoid an even worse outcome. A middle-aged man may decide to cut down on his cholesterol, salt, and sugar intake for the sake of his health. While he does not like having to watch his diet or facing the fact that he is growing older, he chooses to do so in order to live a more healthy and perhaps longer life. These voluntary changes about which we feel ambivalent can be difficult to live with. Deep down we know that there is no one to blame for the decision but ourselves, even while we wish there were.

It is important to remember that, even in changes we did not cause to happen, we still have control over our *response* to the change. When we are fired through no seeming fault of ours, we choose how to react to the firing. No one can take that away from us. The Austrian psychiatrist Viktor Frankl wrote about how he survived a concentration camp in World War II. From that experience he found that the freedom which belongs to all humans and which nobody can take away is the freedom to assume an *attitude* toward what happens to us. [4]

Consider the following situation, in which it would have been easy for Joe to assume that he had no options, when a relationship shifted.

When Joe discovered that Bill, a newcomer at church, enjoyed fishing, they quickly became Saturday fishing buddies. The following spring they went for a long weekend to a lake farther away from home. The ride in the car and the free time in the evenings gave them a chance to talk, and Joe was able to share personally with Bill. Since he had almost no close friends, Joe appreciated this developing relationship.

After the weekend fishing trip, Joe sensed a withdrawal on Bill's part. He seemed less approachable at church and began to turn down invitations to fish with what appeared to be rather weak excuses. Joe's initial reaction was to give up and let the relationship grow apart. As he thought about how much the friendship was coming to mean to him, however, he saw other options besides simply staying quiet. He could choose to say something to Bill and find out what was going on. If Bill was upset about something that happened during their weekend away, perhaps talking directly about it would be a first step in reconciliation. If he had an annoying habit which upset Bill, Joe could decide whether the habit was something he was willing to work to change.

When Joe did share his awareness of a growing distance between them, Bill revealed that his teenage son had been caught smoking marijuana at school and that he and his wife had been preoccupied in dealing with their son and the effect on their family. Bill's more personal sharing deepened their relationship, and Joe was relieved to know that he was not the problem.

Even if he had been the problem and they could not work out a mutually satisfactory solution, Joe, in discussing his concern, would feel better about letting go of the relationship than if he kept quiet. He would find the change easier to handle, knowing he had explored the options. Joe would have felt more in control.

Temporary–Permanent. Changes can also be classified according to whether they are temporary or permanent. In some cases, a change that is temporary may be easier to handle. An acute illness, which the medical doctor assures us we will get over, is very different from a chronic illness or disability. A stay in the hospital, an operation, a limited period of being out of work—all are easier to deal with if it is certain we are going to feel better in the near future.

In other cases, however, a change is easier to adjust to if we know it is likely to be more permanent. A major move to another part of the country may be easier to live with if we know that this is a long-term decision. The permanence of such a change can encourage us to get on with life rather than putting life on hold for a while.

In any case, the temporary or permanent nature of the change is important to the way we handle it. A number of factors, such as our stage in life and the particular kind of change, make a difference as to whether a temporary or a permanent change is easier on us. An involuntary change that is temporary is usually easier than an involuntary change that is permanent. We can deal with a lot of stress or an unhappy situation as long as we know that there is a definite end to it.

Desirable–Undesirable. It goes without saying that the desirability of a change makes a major difference in the way we view and deal with the change. An involuntary change that is pleasing to us is not so bad, even though we would prefer to have control over it.

Most changes involve aspects that are satisfying, while other changes do not. We decide to move into a larger house, which gives our family more space and is in a quieter neighborhood, and after the move we find that the house is everything we hoped it would be. However, we find things we miss about our old house: its "old shoe" feel, the closeness we felt in tripping over each other, the nearness to shopping and schools. And there are adjustments we had not anticipated: It takes longer to commute to work, and the children miss climbing the big tree that was in our old back yard.

Even changes we have chosen, and which are basically good and in our best interest, come with a cost. All of us would like changes which are nice, easy, and free!

Predictable–Unpredictable. In some situations, it helps to be able to predict that a change is on the way. As parents grow older and increasingly frail, we begin to think about options for taking care of them when they are no longer able to care for themselves. There is time to explore alternatives and preferences with them. When the day comes that they are no longer able to live independently, the change is made easier by our planning and anticipation.

If knowing in advance means only that we will worry, it is probably better that we do not know. It would do most of us no good, for example, to know in advance that we are going to have a major illness or accident. But generally, except in those cases where we are helpless, we prefer knowing that a change is on the way. Then we do not have to deal with being surprised or caught off guard as well as dealing with the change itself.

Gradual–Sudden. The length of time it takes for a transition to begin and, once begun, to be completed makes a difference in our response. In some situations and for some persons, the gradual onset of a change makes coping with it easier. In other circumstances and for other people a sudden onset is best. A disaster we know about and can anticipate creates great anxiety and worry. For example, farmers in the Midwest who are losing their farms deal with enormous stress for years as they face lower prices for their crops, borrowing more and more money, not being able to pay it back, and finally filing for bankruptcy.

The response to the gradual/sudden dimension depends on the individual as well as on the situation. Many people say they would prefer a sudden death, for example, while others state they would want to know about it and have a chance to say goodbye.

Personal–Communal. Changes are usually less difficult to deal with if the people around us and the new situation itself are stable. A few years ago I moved to a teaching position in a theological school. The school and the community were fairly stable, so I was supported in adjusting to the new environment. Then recently our faculty and staff offices were moved in the middle of the term to another building. Neither the situation nor the people were stable. This time I was adjusting at the same time as everyone else. There was a comforting sense of comradeship in such a communal change, but my anxiety and stress were compounded at times as I listened to the feelings of faculty, staff, and students who were also in the transition. Likewise, they were often unable to provide support for me. At times, our individual anxiety fed the anxiety of the others.

In the late 1960s and early 1970s, the entire country was in turmoil. Persons who were adolescents during that time now talk about the difficulty of growing up and dealing with personal changes while every institution and every part of society was also in change. What stability they found was interpreted as rigidity and rejection. As these young people discovered, the breadth of the change makes a difference in the way we deal with it, apart from the resources that are at our disposal.

Given the above dimensions, the most difficult transition would be one that happens to us outside our control or ability to predict, has permanent undesirable consequences, and occurs when the community around us is unstable. The sudden or accidental death of a young child while a family is moving to another home would certainly be one of the worst cases. So tragic and enduring is such a loss that one writer believes a parent never stops grieving.[5]

Families and Transitions

A central dimension of all transitions is the effect of the family. "Family" is defined broadly here, to include not only our parents but also other persons with whom we have lived and shared some commitment to the relationship. The family in which we grew up exerts a strong influence upon the way in which we are living through transitions today. The family has provided both resources and liabilities for the process and shapes our responses in ways of which we are not aware.

When one member of a family grows out of a stage, the rest of the family has to adjust to the change. When a child first enters school, the transition affects not only the child but also the parents, especially the one who has been the primary caretaker. The other children also have to adjust. Older siblings already in school may have to adjust to having the younger one now wait for the bus with them and perhaps to guiding her or him at school. Younger siblings will have to get used to not having the now-school-age sibling with them during the day. Obviously, not only the child but also the parents and other children in the family have entered a different stage. The tears that often accompany this transition may signal a kind of unspoken awareness that "things will never be the same." Indeed, they will not.

Sometimes the effect on the family is more direct—changing jobs and moving to another part of the country, for example. Our families move with us and are thrown into transitions individually and as family units. In a more indirect way, an accident causes adjustments not only for the victim but also for the victim's family and close friends. These transitions become overlapping ones, which can either heighten the tension and difficulties for each person or can help each person as they provide mutual support.

Models. The family provided us with models for handling transitions by the way it dealt with various changes in the lives of family members. We saw our parents and other important persons in our childhood deal with change and stress. They provided patterns for responding to transitions, patterns embedded in our bones. Even if they are negative models, we still use those persons as a standard for the way we do *not* want to be. We have no choice but to deal with these important influences that come to us from our past.

Many of us have come to our marriage with inherited models of traditions, roles, structures, and rules concerning family life, specifically concerning change within the context of family life. Our spouses have their own models, which they bring into the relationship. Each of us, out of our separate backgrounds, will then begin to form a relationship that will define itself in terms of new traditions, roles, structures, and rules. If we have not married, we have taken these inbred models into various other close relationships with individuals and groups. We will consciously want some things done just the way they were in our childhood, while other things we will want done differently. The rules and structures that are unspoken or unconscious will exert the most power because they cannot be negotiated.

In terms of the anxiety that goes along with change, our childhood families provided lasting models. As Edwin Friedman shows so well, families develop patterned ways of handling anxiety that affect the whole family system.[6] We learn to deny anxiety, or to blow it out of proportion, or to try to help others with theirs, or to get angry at someone as a way to divert attention, or whatever. As adults we later use these patterns when change and the accompanying anxiety occur. These patterns can be altered with conscious work over time.

Boundaries. "Boundary" is a metaphor for an imaginary line that separates the family from other groups and that separates individuals and subgroups within the family. An effectively functioning family has clear boundaries but not rigid ones. It is important to know who belongs to our family and who does not. A family with weak boundaries is a chaotic family, where people are constantly coming and going. Living in this kind of family makes transitions difficult because there is no stability to hold on to while we are changing.

On the other hand, a family with rigid boundaries has trouble letting the children grow up and leave home. This kind of family tends to stay closely tied together, even though not necessarily living under the same roof, and has difficulty interacting with the world. Transitions are difficult for persons in this type of family because changes are routinely squelched and denied.

Boundaries within the family need to be clear, yet flexible. For example, it needs to be clear as to the way decisions are made and where responsibility lies. The parents should ask for their privacy to be respected, and they should respect the privacy of their children.

Tom grew up as a substitute husband for his mother. His father was often out of town with his job; when he was present he was passive. Tom had little privacy in the house; his mother would enter his room without knocking. As Tom grew older, his mother confided in him. They often shared the same bed when his father was away. Tom ended up marrying a woman who continued to intrude on his time and space. Although he was quite intelligent, he had a great deal of trouble as an adult in knowing who he was and making decisions about his life.

Tom was not prepared for dealing with transitions, given the lack of boundaries in his childhood. He spent years in therapy attempting to work out his identity and to be free to live as he chose.

Rules. The rules families live by make a difference in the way we deal with transitions. Some rules are conscious and talked about aboveboard: how household chores get done, for example. Others are less conscious but exert enormous influence: how conflict is handled, for example. These unconscious norms we can more easily discern as we listen and observe interactions in a family other than our own. The proverbs that get repeated, the things we say to ourselves and to others about our family, and stories that are handed down can be ways of discovering what the rules of the family actually are. When our own children were young, for example, they picked up from us and began saying to each other and to other children, during discussions as well as during arguments, "We are *not* a hitting family!" Rules in the following areas will make a difference in transitions.

"Realness." This area has to do with how real we allow each other to be in our family. Do we have to play a role—of super-parent or superkid, or black sheep, or the smart kid like Uncle Allan, or the shy kid like Aunt Grace? Or can we be who we are, a person with feelings, needs, vulnerabilities, fears, gifts, joys, blind sides? Do we have to pretend in order to be accepted and loved?

Obviously the more okay it is to be real in our family, the easier it will be to pay attention to what is going on inside us and to honor it during a transition. A "real" God speaks to real people and asks for a real response. A real family can help us live that way.

Differences. The unwritten rules about the way differences are handled affect the way we deal with transitions. If everyone in the family is supposed to think and feel and act the same way, then a transition for any individual in that family will be hard to handle successfully. If differences of opinion or anger are to be avoided, then we will have trouble responding to the call of God, which may come from beyond the family and call us to take a different road. Transitions involve us in self-definition, which may mean taking stands that are not agreeable to family and friends.

Traditions. The traditions of a family also make a difference in the way change is handled. Families develop certain rituals that help the members identify themselves as a family and mark the passing of time. Most families have certain traditions at holiday times, for example, which are repeated year after year, with some change as the children grow older and leave. The changes, however, tend to become incorporated as new rituals. Thanksgiving increasingly seems to be a time to return to our families of origin and be together. Vacation time may become ritualized in some families, so that the family always observes it with certain activities.

For our purposes here, traditions are important for the sense of continuity they provide in the midst of transitions. Given all the changes families experience, as units and as individuals within the group, traditions can have ever-increasing significance. Solid, sturdy traditions can provide anchor points in the lives of families.

The Green family had long enjoyed an annual vacation at the beach. As the children grew older and left home, the vacation at the beach became the annual reunion time for everyone. The children, now with their spouses and their own children, make a special effort and drive long distances in order to return for this tradition. The parents stay for an additional week, to enjoy each other after the children and grandchildren are gone. They have thereby acknowledged their new stage of family life, while still maintaining the tradition.

Communication Patterns. The communication patterns in the family will make a difference in the way transitions are talked about and dealt with. Straight communication has to do with actions, feelings, and words matching each other. When we talk straight to each other we each know how the other thinks and feels, even if we do not agree.

The straighter the communication pattern is in the family, the easier it will be to talk to each other during a time of transition. The various feelings and needs of the different people involved can be acknowledged and dealt with. There is, therefore, a greater likelihood that family members can complete each step in the transition process before moving on to the next and that no block will occur.

Blocked communication can be the result of unclear boundaries, not being real with each other, a rule legislating sameness, worshiping the family, or fearing change. Whenever part of ourselves has to be hidden, there is blocked communication. When the communication gets unblocked, transitions are free to proceed.

Unblocking communication is not easy, especially in a family system that tries to maintain stability at any cost. We usually look at our communication patterns only when we are hurting. It may take a therapist to help us begin to talk straight to each other. Once straight communication begins, we can feel freed and exhilarated.

> Bob and Carol's marriage had grown routine, and they had never learned to talk to each other. When Bob discovered that Carol was having an affair, they sought counseling. As Bob began to put words to his anger and pain, he learned how to talk about his feelings. For several months Bob and Carol would stay up at night, talking with each other about their years together, and then about their own childhood experiences.
>
> Bob and Carol had found the excitement of talking straight to each other, and they made up for lost time. Later they used their newfound skill to work through some knots in their relationship. The transition of a divorce was avoided.

Attitude Toward Life. From our parents, we have gained a basic attitude that is located somewhere along the continuum of trust–mistrust and openness–closedness toward life, which includes change. These attitudes toward life, noted here, provide personal resources which can help us deal with transitions.

Trust–Mistrust. Issues of trust and mistrust arise in the first year of life, according to Erik Erikson.[7] There is a continuum between trust and mistrust, so that all of us have some mistrust. If we have no mistrust, we are apt to be gullible and easily manipulated. However, persons who have good parenting in the early years will tend to be more trusting.

Personal change will be easier to deal with if we are more on the trusting side. If we basically trust ourselves, others, God, and the world, then we do not shrink back from change. Trust can help us be open to discern and respond to what we perceive as the call of God to us.

Openness–Closedness. The way in which we feel open or closed toward the world is related to trust. The flexibility of family members to relate and to move away from each other, to move close to each other and to move out into the world, makes a difference in the way we respond to transitions. The way in which our parents opened or did not open their doors to guests, strangers, and visitors gives a good indication of how open they felt toward the world. Within certain boundaries, a flexible openness both to the family and to the outside world makes it easier for us to deal with transitions when they come along.

Attitude Toward Change. These qualities of trust–mistrust and openness–closedness help shape our basic stance toward change. The way in which the family deals with change strongly affects the way transitions are managed. The mistrusting and closed person may hunker down and let change blow over. The trusting and open person will move into change and see it as the call of God to territory where new challenges await and where learning and growing can occur, even though pain and difficulties will also be present. The flexibility of trust and openness can help us bend with change rather than remain rigid and possibly break.

The way in which the family views change becomes crucial for the individual who is undergoing a transition. If we see change as basically bad, we will seek to avoid it. This means that we stick our heads in the ground and hope the change will go away. (In that position we may not hear the call of God!) We will opt for stability and pay the price of losing a journey with God into the unknown where new life can be found.

Some American families seem to see change as the most important value in life. The pace of change has accelerated in our culture to the point that some families appear to embrace it as an idol. Boredom is considered to be the great evil. The newest item on the market, the latest development in technology, the most recent fad—all give meaning to our consumer-oriented life. In this situation, transitions are embraced but not worked through. Endings happen all the time, and beginnings are a dime a dozen. The painful wilderness phase is never acknowledged, and life is lived like a flat stone skimming across the surface of the water.

With the balanced attitude of seeing change as necessary and important, we can take change seriously without either worshiping or avoiding it. The pain of change is acknowledged, as are the potential rewards. If the transition work is done well, we learn that the change is important for our journey. Sometimes we wish there were a different way to learn and grow, but if we have grown up in a family where change is seen as necessary and important, we know how to deal in creative ways with most transitions that come.

Religious Resources. What is the center of worship in the family? For families who worship themselves, the call of God to transition and transformation will be muffled. For families who worship sameness or unreality or stability, a call to change will sound foreign and will be avoided. However, even in those families, the call of God can be heard and responded to. In order to become a whole, separate person in such a family, a member may leave and not return. In other cases, the interactions within the family system are changed in response to God's call. With work, the family *can* change the rules by which it lives and the god it worships.

Mark and Betty found a note from their eleven-year-old daughter, Linda, that said she wanted to kill herself. When they took her to therapy, they discovered that their own high motivation for achievement had been absorbed by Linda, so that she felt she never measured up. With some work, they were able to stop placing that unspoken expectation onto her and begin affirming her as a person. For the first time Linda was able to express her feelings to her parents, and they were able to hear her.

Over time, Mark and Betty were able to change some of the family rules about the value of achievement and about conflict. The family functioned better with the change, and Linda was able to make a smoother transition into adolescence.

We bring with us from our past the religious practices of our childhood. Even if we have long ago ceased such practices, or forgotten them, they are still present and available, especially if we are feeling desperate. People who have not prayed since they said bedtime prayers as a child will find themselves talking to God—perhaps bargaining with God—during a major transition. The bedtime prayer may run through our minds at such times. People who stopped attending religious services upon leaving their parents' home will find themselves slipping into the back pew of a church during a crisis.

Hymns connected to important events in our past provide a resource for comfort and stability when we are going through times of upset and confusion. Hymns speak to our souls in ways that bypass our intellectual sophistication. Other rituals, such as occur in more liturgical churches, can provide the same comfort and stability if they were part of our childhood.

Multiple Transitions. While each transition produces stress simply because of the changes involved, the stress can become unmanageable when two or more transitions overlap. A person who is involved in extensive rehabilitation after being seriously injured in an automobile accident, and who then learns that a parent has suddenly died, may be thrown into a severe crisis. The stress can also become unmanageable when we go through a developmental transition at the same time one of our children or spouse is also going through a transition. Mid-life often arrives at the same time that one of our children becomes an adolescent. On those occasions we need outside support and help.

One of the most difficult times for a family is when several transitions are occurring at the same time. When one person is going through a transition, the family can usually handle the ripple effects. When two persons are going through separate transitions, however, the stress on the family begins to mount.

Ann, a senior, was getting ready to attend her high school graduation ceremony when her father received a phone call notifying him that he was being offered a new job. He had been looking for a position with new challenges and opportunities after a decade in his present job. The job he was offered was one he was excited about and seemed to be an answer to his prayers. If he accepted, however, it meant that they would have to move to another state.

Ann's elementary and high school years had all been spent in the same community. She enjoyed school, had many friends there, and made good grades. At the graduation service Ann could not figure out whether her tears were because she was graduating and leaving her friends for college, or because her parents and home were leaving her. Three years later, as she entered her senior year in college, she began to recall the feelings and turmoil of that summer and recognize how much it had affected her. As she shared her feelings with her family, they too went back and talked about those difficult days of transition, and the fact that so much was going on. Her older sister had recently moved out of the house to live on her own; her father was in the process of career reevaluation; her parents were moving to another state. This was too much to process at the time, so it came up again later.

As Ann and her family discovered, multiple transitions may mean that everything cannot be dealt with at the time. We are sturdy creatures, however, and unfinished feelings will wait for an opportune time. We do not have to feel guilty if we are not able to handle all the changes. We can know that adjusting to them will be spread out over time, and we will have a chance to deal with some of the feelings later, if they are important.

A network of friends can be helpful when several changes are going on at the same time. In addition to their emotional support, friends can help with some of the things we do not have time or energy to accomplish.

Developmental Transitions

A special category of transitions has to do with the normal stages of development we all traverse. These transitions are usually involuntary and of a permanent nature. They may or may not be desirable and are probably more personal than communal (although our spouse or friends may be in the same stage because of their age). Even though children change most obviously in size and ability, it is now clear that adults also continue to go through stages as they age.

In a study of men, Daniel Levinson found that relatively stable periods of life, lasting six to eight years, alternated with periods of transition. The fundamental tasks of "a transitional period are to question and reappraise the existing structure, to search for new possibilities in self and world, and to modify the present structure enough so that a new one can be formed."[8] A comparable study has not yet been done with women. It is possible that the stages are somewhat different for females and may extend for different periods of time.

Popular literature in this area is helping us to be more aware of these changes that occur as we age. Each new stage of life requires giving up some comfortable patterns and being open to moving into a new place. For example, growing older requires more attention to diet and exercise. We cannot get away with abusing our bodies and still feel good. This kind of change requires work.

Most of us feel better about these developmental transitions when we discover that what we are going through is normal. While not removing the necessity of doing the personal inner work, knowing that we are not going crazy or that something is not necessarily wrong with us allows us to bear the anxiety more easily. In addition, the reassurance that others are also having similar experiences has a powerful effect. Consider Sally's experience.

Sally came to see me one day feeling depressed and worried. She was a successful career woman with a promising future. Her work had been of primary importance; she had shown little interest in men and consequently had not married. In recent weeks she found herself thinking about the fact that her childbearing years were disappearing. Reevaluating her priorities, she began to think about her unmarried status. She had been happy in her life up to this point and thought that the issues of marriage and children were settled in her life.

When she told me that she was twenty-nine years old, I assured her that the issues of marriage and children tend to emerge for many unmarried women in our society around age thirty. Greatly relieved, Sally was then able to proceed with the personal work she needed to do. Over time Sally came to see that closing off the option of marriage was a result of an unhappy and damaged childhood, which included living with parents who constantly fought with each other. A successful career provided important self-esteem, and she did not have to deal with intimate relationships. As she became aware of her childhood wounds, reexperienced them, and shared them in a trusting relationship, she experienced healing. Then she was able to relate to other people more easily and make decisions about a committed relationship with a man.

What Is at Stake?

When we sail easily through some changes, yet others cause us great difficulty, we begin to wonder what makes the difference. For example, a friend of mine seems to change places of residence without any trouble, yet she has a lot of difficulty when one of her children grows up and leaves home. What is at stake when some changes are hard while others are relatively easy? The following are possibilities.

Personal Investment. Our personal investment in the area where change is occurring certainly makes a difference. My friend simply invests little in a home but a great deal in her children. Obviously, when change occurs in a part of our life where we have little at stake, the change is easy.

Need for Security. We have varying needs for security and order in our lives. When these security needs get shaken, we begin to feel it; our foundations begin to shake, and we fear they might crumble. Our needs for security are greater in some periods of life than in others. Another friend reported that after his children were born he found himself taking fewer risks when skiing.

Unhealed Areas. Unhealed areas from the past affect the way we live in the present. When we are having difficulty dealing with a transition, even after we have worked on it, we may wonder if some hurt from our past is mixed in the problem. In the example of the friend with a lot of difficulty letting her children leave home, she may have unresolved issues about when *she* left her parents' home. In dealing with her children's growing up and leaving, she may be at the same time dealing with the earlier issue with her parents. The stakes are high, but they can be lowered by separating the issues and working on each one individually. (This is easier said than done!)

Identity. Our identity is especially tied to certain parts of our lives. When change begins to affect the way we see ourselves, we feel the pain. Persons who retire find how much their jobs mean to them. In some cases, their sense of who they are is invested in their jobs and in being productive. Now that they are no longer working, they have to face themselves in a way they did not have to as long as they were working. They may not know who they are apart from their jobs, so they become depressed. Perhaps that is the reason for higher rates of physical illness and suicide after retirement.

For all of us, our identity is tied to our roles, our daily routines, our lifestyle. When any of these dimensions of our life changes, then our sense of who we are, our identity, is affected. The result can be profound anxiety. We may feel that we are losing our grip. Along with the anxiety go fear, pain, and anger. The way we deal with all these feelings is a major determining factor in the way we move through a transition, learn from it, get stuck in it, or retreat from it.

Belief System. Our belief system and philosophy of life are the deepest levels at which we can be touched. When a young child dies, we grieve for the expectation that *we* were going to die before our children. We also are confronted with the fact that we were not able to protect our children from pain. That can deeply shake our beliefs about ourselves and our role as parents.

When a parent dies, we have to confront the fact that we are never going to get what we feel we needed. Belief in the world as a fair place may be thrown into question.

Relationship with God. Our personal relationship with God and beliefs about God can be threatened. This can occur in several areas.

The Way God Acts. First, the way we were taught that God acts may be called into question. Children often assume (or were taught) that, like a good parent, God rewards good people and punishes the bad. As adults we may live all our life with the belief that if we are a "good" Christian or Jew or whatever, and do the right things, God will be good to us. When something bad happens, we naturally begin to examine our lives to see why we deserve it. At some point in a major crisis we may ask, "Why did God let this happen to me?" If we can find nothing to warrant God's punishment, we begin to question the way God acts. Does God act as God wants, without any regard for our situation?

Who God Is. Second, our view of God's character may be called into question. When our child dies, or our marriage breaks up, or we develop a chronic illness, we may question our assumptions about God and wonder if God is good. Is God basically good or cruel? Does God care?

Our Relationship with God. Third, our relationship with God has to be reexamined. If God acts differently from our expectation, and we wonder about God's character, we are going to wonder if we can trust God. As trust becomes an issue, the very foundation of our relationship to God is called into question. Why pray or turn to a God whom we are not sure we can trust?

Deep anger and disappointment, hurt, and feeling lost are common during this time. In our anger and bitterness, we may secretly feel sorry that we refrained from doing bad or selfish things all those years and may begin to break loose and do those things now.

The reworking of our relationship to God can move us into a deeper connection with the real God behind the "God" of our childhood or the "God" of the easy years of our adulthood. It is also possible in our disappointment to turn away from God and become apathetic. If the "God" of our childhood has to be given up, we may not engage in the hard work of discovering the true God.

Rather than change our relationship we can compartmentalize our God, so that real issues in our daily living do not affect our worship. Our God remains in a closet, to be brought out only on stated occasions, then carefully put away. The attraction of this position is that our spiritual life is not dirtied by the daily struggles of living. While this alternative may be necessary for a while because of limitations of energy, the cost is that our relationship with God stops growing and stops being relevant to our daily life.

For Personal Reflection

Depict your life with its progressive changes as a line on a graph with two axes. On the east-west, or horizontal, axis, mark the passing of time from birth to the present, with dates or your age as reference points. Your lifeline graph will look like this:

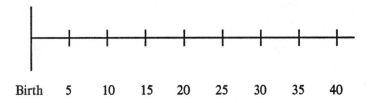

Birth   5   10   15   20   25   30   35   40

Draw a longer lifeline than is shown here and extend it to your present age, so that you have room to record the major turning points. To get the most out of this exercise, you will need to invest time and energy.

Recall experiences that were important to your formation or that were turning points. On the north-south, or vertical, axis, note whether each event you marked on the horizontal axis was positive or negative by placing a mark either above the horizontal line or below. A word or two written by the mark will help you recall the experience. The intensity of the experience can be noted by how far up or down on the vertical axis you place the mark. As you connect the marks with a line, you get a picture of the pattern of transitions in your life.

As you look at your lifeline and the transitions, note the different dimensions of the transitions:

> controlled/uncontrolled
> gradual/sudden
> personal/communal
> temporary/permanent
> desirable/undesirable
> predictable/unpredictable
> personal/communal

For the more important parts of transition, looking at the developmental stage you were in at the time and and influence of your family may help you understand how you experienced those times.

What was at stake for you in each of the major changes?

3

The First Phase:
Endings

There is plenty we have to give up in order to grow. For we cannot deeply love anything without becoming vulnerable to loss. And we cannot become separate people, responsible people, connected people, reflective people without some losing and leaving and letting go.

—**Judith Viorst**[1]

William Bridges, in *Transitions: Making Sense of Life's Changes,* describes the three phases of transitions as ending, the neutral zone, and the new beginning. The following three chapters will look at each phase in detail, expand on this concept, and ground it in a religious framework.

How Endings Occur

One day while I was sitting in my office it suddenly occurred to me that I would not be doing that particular job the rest of my life. I was not especially unhappy doing what I was doing. In fact, I received real satisfaction from my work and believed that I was good at it. Later I saw that this revelation was the first sign of an ending for me.

God has made us to be creatures who grow and change. Because we are created, our lives have a beginning and an end. In between those two points we are in transition. Transitions are built into the order of creation and are an organic part of our lives.

The first step in any internal transition or deep change is an ending. We may not control when the ending occurs or how it happens to us. Even when we exert control—by deciding to change jobs, move, buy a new car, or terminate a relationship, for example—something has ended inside us before we make that decision. Our action stems from the decision emerging from this internal ending.

If we make external changes before this internal ending has occurred and been recognized, we may find it difficult to become committed to the new situation. Our bodies may express this incomplete ending in a variety of ways: difficulty sleeping, low energy, mild aches and pains, feeling below par, preoccupation, or irritability.

An internal ending is most likely to occur gradually. As we become aware of an ending in process, certain events or occasions of awareness take on a symbolic value for us. A husband who described something as the "last straw" was describing an event that had symbolic value in his life. A woman who had been interim minister for two years left on her summer vacation knowing that she would not have the energy to return and begin a third fall of activities in her church. And I can still clearly remember my office as the place where it occurred to me that I would not spend the rest of my life in that particular job. The "last straw" of the spouse, the implications of going on vacation for the interim minister, and the insight in my office all marked endings in our lives.

A number of feelings cluster around such an event which result in our admission that an ending has indeed begun to occur. The symbolic event then serves to coalesce our emerging awareness and provides a way for us to talk about what has happened to us.

Denial

While there is some overlap, a true beginning cannot be achieved until an ending has been completed. Our culture does not encourage us to pay attention to our endings and to the grief they cause. People often brag about leaving one job on Friday and beginning a new one on Monday. It's as though we are dashing headlong on a horse in one direction. While in midstride, we jump onto another horse and dash off in a different direction without taking the time to disentangle from the reins. We do not consider the reasons for changing horses or our feelings about the first horse and the direction in which we were riding. The danger is that we will never become attached to the new horse and never become committed to the new direction.

If this denial of internal endings becomes a pattern, our life-style can become one of floating through life without roots. Nothing seems to matter except some external and culturally sanctioned signs of success—such as money, cars, houses, clothes, children, or office location and furnishings. With change occurring so rapidly in our society, it becomes easy to deny the work that change entails and just "go with the flow." People change spouses like buying a new pair of shoes, join a church like shopping for a pleasing restaurant, and change jobs simply for more money. To have and to consume take top priority in our lives.

On the other hand, denial of an internal ending may mean that we stay where we are. If we are not aware of a shift that happens inside us, we can remain in a relationship, stay in a job, continue with external values and a lifestyle that are not within God's call. The internal questioning and bubbling can be dismissed as the result of what we ate for dinner. It can be ignored by getting busy with other things and distracting ourselves.

The price we pay for this approach is a vague dissatisfaction with life that hits us at odd moments: trying to go to sleep at night, standing in line for a movie and imagining the people laughing and talking are happier than we are, night dreaming, being bothered by aches and pains so that we end up in the doctor's office, living with a mild depression that we assume is part of living and growing older, attempting to lose weight and realizing that eating is filling a void in our lives. Is the addiction in our society—to relationships, sex, alcohol, food of various kinds, drugs of both legal and illegal kinds, television—partially a consequence of our inner emptiness and the resulting unacknowledged hunger?

Our refusal to face an internal ending can be self-conscious and even deliberate. To face an ending and its implications for our life requires hard work that can be upsetting. The price of dealing openly with an ending can appear so high that we shrink back. However, the price of not dealing with the ending must also be calculated. It is paid on the installment system, over a long period of time, with detrimental consequences to our bodies, relationships, and spiritual life. On the other hand, plunging into an ending puts the cost at the front end, in terms of dealing with loss and grief.

In the following case, Bert found himself wrestling with the cost of ending his job versus the cost of not ending it.

Bert came for counseling because he felt insecure in his relationship with his wife and was jealous when they got together with another couple and she talked with the man. In addition to the marital problem, he was also unhappy with his bureaucratic job. His creative side had no outlet, and his joy in working with young people and his need to feel that he was making a contribution to society were not being expressed in his eight-to-five work. However, the position paid well and had excellent benefits. Bert had children who would be going to college in a few years, and he intended to support them financially. In addition, it was important, because of his own chaotic childhood, that he provide a stable home for his family.

Bert concluded that it was best to stay in his job, even though he was unhappy there and was having to work hard to keep up his efficiency level. He left counseling before it became clear whether his marriage was going to survive. He opted for stability now, with the possibility of a marriage break-up later on, rather than face the guaranteed upset that a job change and lower income would cause in the short run. He lived with a fairly high level of anxiety, because he did not know if he would end up losing his marriage and family, the very things he was so intent on maintaining.

Bert was in a real bind. As he looked at his options and the cost of each, he chose to stay where he was and ignore his job dissatisfaction. The mental cost of a denial such as Bert's is a loss of alertness. The challenge of new things and dealing with new problems is no longer present. Our mind turns to what we are going to do after work today, or this weekend, or next vacation, or the big one: retirement. We then find our pleasure primarily around the edges of our job and in plans for the future.

The emotional cost of such a denial can be boredom and a low-level depression. The zest for living seems to disappear, and new clothes or a new relationship or a vacation only temporarily lifts our spirits. In terms of the physical cost, the weakest part of our body seems to express the repressed problems. It is also easy to forget to take care of our bodies, so we end up eating and drinking too much, not paying attention to a balanced diet and exercise, which of course makes our bodies more vulnerable to stress and disease.

In addition to the physical, mental, and emotional results of denying an ending, the spiritual price is a loss of a sense of purpose in life. We find ourselves relying instead on finding meaning in small, external parts of life, such as vacations, eating out, and parties. Bert, who stayed in his job for the sake of stability for his children, was apparently finding meaning in providing for his children in a way in which he himself had not been provided for. If his children refused to go to college, there would clearly be a crisis in the family, and his meaning in life would be threatened.

The Call of God

The spiritual issue in dealing with endings is hearing and responding to the call of God. The scriptures, and the lives of religious persons throughout history, have given witness to God's calling persons into new places. As God called Abraham, God calls us: "Leave your country, your kindred and your father's house for a country which I shall show you" (Gen. 12:1). It is common to speak of the spiritual life as one of pilgrimage. As Lewis Sherrill notes, a pilgrim is a person who is on a quest.[2] The goal may be a shrine, as in the Middle Ages, or a land where the pilgrim can live out personal values and political ideals, as in the first centuries of this country. The quest includes body, mind, and spirit but must begin with spirituality sensitivity. In order to launch ourselves on such a quest, we must feel called. Some people experience a burning desire, a consuming passion. God may be the one who gives that desire, or passion, as part of the call into new territory. Others experience a more low-key impulse to pursue a particular direction. It is a common struggle to ascertain what God's call to us really is.

Care has to be taken to discern the call of God from neurotic needs within ourselves. A burning desire that could be interpreted as a call from God should be tested with others who know us well, with the community of faith, and through prayer and honest reflection. The persistence over time of a burning desire indicates that it must be taken seriously. What may first appear to be a call from God may turn out to be a flight from intimacy, a fear of commitment, or a strong need for blessing or approval. The issue of discernment is discussed later in this chapter.

God's call comes not only to heroes—men and women who do great things—but to every person in every time and every place. The call may or may not be to leave a place physically or do something dramatic. Some people whom Jesus met asked to accompany him, but he told them to stay and witness and work in their own places. In heeding God's call, all outward appearances of our life may remain the same. The inner meaning and the motivating reasons will be different, however, because they will now derive from God's call rather than just from our own needs and desires.

The call of God is at the heart of a Christian's vocation, a word which comes from a Latin word that means "calling." The vocation of the Christian is to live in response to the call of God. The call of God for us is to be in partnership in continuing the act of creation. We are to become co-creators with God. "There are a vast number of opportunities for partnership in God's work in the world; there is no shortage of significant ways to be part of the divine action."[3]

At the point in life where we hear God's call, we must look at the internal and external endings required to make an adequate response. Abraham's call appeared to supersede everything else. In following that call, Abraham made major changes in the way he was living, which must have meant a real shift in his identity. A number of endings were necessary as he went about preparing to pull up stakes and journey to a distant place. The same thing occurs when we hear the call of God.

Perhaps more common today is to experience an ending or

change first and then to search for the new thing God may be calling us to do. We feel a deep yearning, but we do not know exactly what to do to meet that yearning. We may be vaguely dissatisfied with our present status and feel that God is calling us to something else, but we do not know what it is.

Risk is involved whenever we hear God's call. We are asked to give up something, to experience an ending, and we may be called to move into an unknown future. Even Abraham, with a clear call from God, did not know the details of what was going to happen or where he was going. Our response to God's call requires taking one step at a time. Through our risking one step, God gives light for the next. When responding to God's call, we find ourselves supplied with the gifts and abilities with which to accomplish the work.

The point is that when we respond to God's call, it always involves an ending. Before moving on, we first have to say goodbye to the place where we have been. If we refuse to listen and respond to God's call, we shrink back from challenge and growth. We draw the circle of our life smaller, and we live on the human level without consideration for the vertical dimension of faith.

I am convinced that as we grow older it becomes increasingly important to be attentive to God's call. It is easy to settle for what we have, to give up our dreams and hopes, to blot out our sense of vision for life and what it can be. At that point, we begin to die emotionally and spiritually.

The Call of God in Mid-Life

The crisis of mid-life may be at bottom one of choosing life or death. By mid-life, most middle-class Americans have gained a certain amount of community status, prestige, and job perks. Family responsibilities are usually heaviest at that time, with teenage children who may be considering college. Can we be open to hearing God's call to a new territory? If we hear can we respond, given what we have to lose? If we do not, a slow process of pulling back, shutting down, playing it safe, living for retirement, or fantasizing some pie-in-the-sky future becomes the guiding norm. The result is a kind of slow, eroding death. While

God can still break in, and transformation can occur at any age,
it becomes increasingly difficult to make major changes after
middle age, especially if our previous pattern has been one of
playing it safe.

The author of the book of Hebrews writes about the temptation to draw back:

> *My upright person will live through faith*
> *but if he [or she] draws back, my soul will take no pleasure. . . .*

> We are not the sort of people who *draw back,* and are lost by it;
> we are the sort who keep *faith* until our souls are saved.
>
> Only faith can guarantee the blessings that we hope for, or
> prove the existence of realities that are unseen.
>
> Hebrews 10:38–11:1

The crises of middle age are intensified by the normal crisis
of meaning which occurs during that time. Much writing in
recent years has reminded us of what often happens around the
mid-point in life. We become more aware of our mortality, and
we begin to think of how many more years of active life remain.
Our parents are growing old, developing infirmities, and dying.
Some friends are struck down in their prime. In small but insis-
tent ways our own bodies remind us of the aging process: they
do not recover as quickly from the strains of overexercise, eating
too much, or going without enough sleep; our muscles lose their
tone; our hair begins to gray; our teeth begin to cause difficulty.
My mid-life crisis began when I chipped my tooth eating pop-
corn!

The early years of our lives have been spent in growing,
exploring the world and ourselves, learning to relate to others,
separating from parents and learning to be independent and
then interdependent. The challenge of these issues can perhaps
carry us through those years. What is going to carry us through
a gradual disintegration of our bodies and an awareness of
death? No wonder our religious faith becomes central at this
time of life! Whether it is conscious and verbalized or not, we
work out some kind of philosophy or faith that helps us either
to face or to avoid the last half of life. If we are open to hearing
God's call, the last half of life will be even more full of life and
perspective, of risk-taking and growth, of change and challenge.

We have nurtured and tended our personal garden for the first thirty or forty years. We have set out many kinds of plants and cared for them. Past mid-life we can enjoy the full flowering of what has been planted, perhaps the harvesting of some crops, which contributes to a feeling of fulfillment and happiness. Just as important, we now have the time and space to experiment and try some new plants, include some hybrids, or even to transplant our garden to distant soil! We may become aware of the unequal distribution of land and resources in the world and feel called to work for change in basic allocations. We may become aware of the threat of nuclear annihilation of the planet and feel called to work for peace and justice. We may become aware of the way we abuse the environment, and feel called to sound the alarm and work for new laws. After all, what do we have to lose? We are going to lose our life in the end, plus all the *things* we have accumulated. If our security is in God, we are more free to heed God's call to live life on the edge.

I have dealt in some detail with mid-life because that is where I am. God calls us as we enter any new developmental stage. As we deal with any transition of a personal and significant nature in our lives, God is in the center, the turning point, calling us to leave the familiar and to travel to a new and strange land. One writer describes his experience of God in a compelling way:

> I keep thinking it is an awesome thing to look into the face of the living God. I feel God is turning the screws so I will get into an ultimate position of transition, but I also feel that *the centre of the circle is buoying me up* [emphasis mine], holding me in suspension as though I were in God's hands. And God, terrible and loving, is with me now in [God's] presence.[4]

The Call of God in Unwanted Transitions

The most difficult transitions to deal with, and to find the call of God in, are the ones we neither choose nor want. I do not believe God causes suffering or brings traumatic transitions upon us. I believe, however, that suffering can be an occasion for growth and self-deepening if we discover and heed the call of God in that situation. God is at work in every situation for purposes of ultimate redemption and reconciliation. We can choose to join God in that work, or to go our own way and miss an opportunity for learning and discipleship. Consider Eleanor's experience as she struggled with tragedy in her family.

Eleanor came for counseling when her teenage daughter was taken to the hospital for attempted suicide. A devout person, Eleanor was committed to her church and was a leader there. She was totally surprised by her daughter's action and began to question what was going on in her family and in her own life. Then she discovered that the suicide attempt was brought on by her husband's sexual advances toward her daughter. There was a long period of dealing with the legal system, moving her family into an apartment, dealing with her own and her children's feelings about what had happened, and dealing with the realization that her church sided with her husband. As she struggled to find meaning in her situation, she got angry with God. She had always tried to be a good person and live a Christian life. She felt that God and her church had let her down. She began attending another church.

As she worked through the many logistical problems and daily issues that arose out of this transition, she began to look at herself. She recognized that from childhood she had been a strong caretaker who denied her own needs and took care of other people. People at church did not know how to relate to her, a person who had always been so strong but now was needy. As she became more aware of her own needs and feelings she became more comfortable in acknowledging them, first to herself and then to others. Relationships with her children and her friends began to be more reciprocal for the first time. She got to know her daughter in a close and loving way as a result of long, hard work on their relationship.

While she never would have chosen such a painful trauma to learn from, she began to see that she was being called to a deeper relationship with herself, with others around her, and with God. In describing her experience to a church group, she summed up her perception the following way: "We have been badly hurt, at very deep levels, in many ways. We are angry and distrustful. My older children still profess belief in God (possibly to make me feel better) but want nothing to do with Christian communities. I am here because I can see God moving through all that has happened. Too many supportive people were met, or things occurred at just the right time, under just the right circumstances, to merely be chance. We have been cared for and guided along this horrendous path we are traveling."

Helps Along the Way

Following are specific suggestions that you may find helpful as you struggle with an ending in your life.

Paying Attention. The crucial requirement in living with endings is to pay attention to them. If we do not, they will slip by us unnoticed or unheeded. We will have missed their meaning, the call of God that is present in the ending.

To pay attention to an ending means more than noting it and living through it. If we treat an ending like a wild roller-coaster ride, where we grit our teeth, hang on for dear life, and look forward to the moment when we will step onto solid ground, then we will have missed the meaning for ourselves. To pay attention to an ending means, first of all, to be open to recognizing an ending when it occurs. In order to be open, we must have the faith that an ending does not mean the ending of everything. We must have faith that God will not put on us more than we can bear. We must remember both in our head and in our gut that endings are part of life, not to be avoided but to be learned from.

To pay attention to an ending is to look beneath the surface, to struggle with the meaning of the situation. God's call may not be readily apparent. We may need to sit with the situation for a while, resisting the temptation to move too quickly to decisions and external endings, until the waters clear and we sense what is at the bottom of our feelings and perceptions.

Curiosity and Patience. Curiosity and patience are important ingredients at this stage and at each succeeding stage. Curiosity

provides a certain amount of distance that helps us not to identify so totally with the current situation that we feel stuck. With
some objectivity, we can see a wider range of options and perhaps even laugh at ourselves. Curiosity can put us in the position
of a student who can learn from the processes going on inside
as well as from the situation. Becoming curious means that we
can let go of some of our need to control.

Patience is important so that we do not move on too quickly
and miss either the griefwork or the learning. The process takes
time, and we do not control it. Patience can prevent us from
aborting or bypassing the process.

Sharing. When wrestling with the meaning of an ending, it is
important to share our struggle with trusted friends and family,
as well as with a pastor or a trained counselor. Isolating ourselves during this time of struggle and discernment will deprive
us of the insights and resources of the community, through
which God also speaks. At times God's call may be heard only
through the voices of others.

Time for Self. Taking time and space for meditation, reflection, prayer, and scripture reading is important in the middle of
an ending. A private retreat at a place designed for that may be
very helpful. Journal-writing may help to clarify where we are
in our lives. Some people find long walks in the woods or by the
seashore helpful. You will have to see what works for you. The
important thing is to take the time and energy to attend to the
ending.

This means changing our usual way of doing things, and
altering our daily routines. If we continue in the same old way
we will deny this new thing that we perceive to have happened
to us and will eventually squelch its voice. Then we can be
tempted to assume that it was only a temporary blip on the
internal radar screen, and we were right to ignore it. We missed
a call to new life.

Paying Attention to Feelings of Grief. When we pay attention to an ending, we soon become aware of feeling grief. We are

losing something—status, income, security of the familiar, comfortable and nurturing relationships. An ending does not mean that what we are leaving was bad for us, although it may become bad for us if we continue in the situation rather than ending it. It may have been the right place or thing for us at that point in our lives. We are being asked to give up that goodness, to say goodbye to it, as we move on. In order to do that, we must grieve.

Grief is the emotional mechanism through which we deal with loss. *There simply is no loss without grief.* We can refuse to grieve and thereby deny the loss and the accompanying feelings. In that case, the ending really does not occur emotionally. An honest new beginning is then not possible. The grief is stored away in the recesses of our psyche and will pop out at a time when we least expect it. Unresolved grief can affect future relationships, our physical health, and our response to God.

The goal of grief is to deal with the variety of feelings associated with loss so that the reality of the loss can be acknowledged, a new beginning can be made, and a faith, altered by the loss, can be reshaped. Through the entire process we can be led by God's Spirit.

The shape and intensity of our grief will depend on the kind of loss with which we are dealing and by the different dimensions involved in the transitions, which were given in chapter 2. For example, the grief over a job change which we chose will be different from the grief over the sudden death of a spouse. After a major loss we find ourselves being sad and feeling both the internal and the external emptiness left by the loss. It's as though part of ourselves has been ripped away, and we are left feeling exposed, vulnerable, lonely, and missing what is now gone. Healing of the emotional tissue needs to occur, and this takes time and caring attention. We may experience a variety of feelings—including pain, depression, anger, and guilt—more intensely than usual. We may act differently from the way we usually do. Sometimes we may find ourselves denying the loss and trying to return to the safe past. At other times we imagine ourselves past this difficult time and into a new, secure place. Jumping back to the past and forward to the future are ways of giving ourselves a break from the grief, before we return to the present work.

The loss can be made into a cherishable memory. Part of griefwork is to make the lost attachments into a memory that can be recalled and affirmed as part of our history. "Working on a memory is like creating an internal emotional scrapbook."[5] The vision of a future time when the grief is finished can provide hope and thereby energize us for the painful work necessary to get to that new place.

C. S. Lewis, a well-known Christian writer, lost his wife to cancer. In dealing with his grief, Lewis wrote in notebooks, which were later published. He describes vividly the feelings connected with raw grief, the

> mad words, the bitter resentments, the fluttering in the stomach, the nightmare unreality, the wallowed-in tears. For in grief nothing "stays put." One keeps on emerging from a phase, but it always recurs. Round and round. Everything repeats. Am I going in circles, or dare I hope I am on a spiral?[6]

Lewis's question at the end is important. Many descriptions of the grief process assume a linear progression from one stage of grief to another. The actual reality of grief, however, may be experienced more as a spiral, where we circle around to a spot directly above the original loss, and reexperience the initial pain, but at a place more removed. Again, C. S. Lewis expresses this process well:

> Sorrow, however, turns out to be not a state but a process. . . . Grief is like a long valley, a winding valley where any bend may reveal a totally new landscape. As I've already noted, not every bend does. Sometimes the surprise is the opposite one; you are presented with exactly the same sort of country you thought you had left behind miles ago. That is when you wonder whether the valley isn't a circular trench. But it isn't. There are partial recurrences, but the sequence doesn't repeat.[7]

Although it never entirely goes away, if we express the grief in its many phases, we find ourselves over time gaining some distance and perspective. The pain is less acute, and we feel ready to move on. However, as a friend of mine says, it is like arthritis: When it rains, it's going to hurt

Paying Attention to Our Bodies. In dealing with an ending, we need to pay attention to our bodies. In fact, our bodies may be the first communicator of an ending. If we listen, our bodies may reveal that things are out of balance, that a change has occurred, or that something is wrong. If we ignore the physical signals, the bodily dis-ease can develop into illness that we will be unable to ignore. However, if the physical illness is treated from only a medical and biological standpoint, we may continue to miss the underlying reason for the problem and thereby miss what we need to learn.

The incarnation in the New Testament refers to the belief that God became a human being in the person of Jesus. For Christians, incarnation means that we have a religion that is located *in the body.* It is to our detriment, and contrary to the biblical witness, to assume that spirituality has to do with only the mind and not the body. In denying the importance of our bodies, we lose our connectedness to other bodies and to all of creation.

We are out of touch with our bodies. As long as we are reasonably healthy we take them for granted. When we get sick, we want the medical doctor to "fix" our bodies. As we take a car that needs to be repaired to the garage, we take our body to the hospital for occasional repairs. Then we put our body back out on the road until it stops running again.

When medical science runs out of magic, we can search for quack remedies or we can begin to listen to the messages our body gives. Listening to our bodies is a discipline that has to be cultivated. Regular prayer, meditation, and gentle exercise can be helpful in learning how to listen. Yoga is an excellent method for "body listening" that contains centuries of wisdom.

If you want to become more aware of your body, you can start by doing the following exercise:

Lie on your back, perhaps with a pillow under your knees, so that you are comfortable. Relax for a moment and become aware of your breathing. Beginning with the top of your head, tense, then relax, each set of muscles throughout your body until you come to your toes. Then let your mind slowly wander back up through your body. When your attention comes to any place which is still tense, speak to that part of your body. Thank it for working so hard for you and appreciate it for what it has been doing. Then tell it that it can let go and relax now. Proceed up through your body until you reach your head. Remain on your back for a while, just relaxing and being at one with yourself.

If you find parts of your body that are tense and do not seem to relax after several times of doing this exercise, you may want to attend a workshop on body relaxation, enroll in a yoga class, or perhaps do some reading on the subject before you proceed further. A good introduction that contains a variety of exercises is Anthony de Mello's *Sadhana: A Way to God, Christian Exercises in Eastern Form.*

If we pay attention, the wisdom of our bodies will continue to guide us through the experience of an ending. If we listen to the language of our bodies and attempt to understand it, we will be guided into healthy ways of treating our bodies. Discomfort in a specific area of our body can also reveal where we need to focus our care and attention. In doing that, we may discover feelings and memories connected with that part of our body. Working with these feelings and memories then becomes part of the work of an ending.

In the following case, Jim found himself forced to listen to his body and to what it was saying concerning the way he was living.

After experiencing a heart attack at age thirty-six, Jim examined his lifestyle. He realized he lived in order to climb the ladder of success, while depriving his wife and children of his time and emotional availability. In the long months of recuperation, he stopped smoking, changed his diet, began to attend church in a more intentional way, and came into counseling to look at his hard-driving, achievement-oriented behavior. He discovered from his childhood some areas that needed healing and, from his adolescence, the way he had cut off his father.

After some exploration of this issue in counseling, Jim was able to talk to his father and experience reconciliation with him. He began to understand that his motive for working so hard had been to prove his worth to his father and earn his approval, even though at conscious levels he had cut off his relationship.

While recovering from the heart attack, Jim was unable to work. His family, friends, and church members supported him during those difficult days. Though it was hard, he allowed them to love him. In turn, he felt for the first time lovable for who he was, rather than for what he did. He began to feel better about himself than he ever had before.

Then a promising new job came along that required him to be on the road a lot. He suddenly dropped out of counseling and I did not hear from him again.

Was he able to maintain his newfound insights and learn from the strong language of a heart attack? If not, his body could have another heart attack or find other ways to express its dis-ease.

Using Our Minds. Our minds are morally neutral and are in the service of our will and our basic orientation to life. As a result, our intellectual processes can be used to deny and cover up an ending, so that life can proceed as usual. Our minds can be quite persuasive in arguing that the ending really did not occur, or that it was really small and so requires no real change or grieving from us.

Endings we do not choose and do not want to go through are the kind we are most likely to use our minds to ignore. The pain of death or divorce can be so great that we use our minds to block out the pain. We have no control over the fact that the event occurred, so we may try to exercise whatever control we can in the way we go through it. Consider the following case:

Jean was doing well after her husband left and divorced her. Even though she wanted to save the marriage, once her husband decided he wanted out she proceeded to see an attorney to protect her interests and to get on with her life. Months later she found herself in a painful relationship with another man and decided to ask for help. As she looked inside, she began to notice how she had controlled herself through the separation and divorce. As Jean allowed herself to "feel her feelings," she discovered that she was so angry at her husband for leaving that she was determined not to let him—or even herself—see that she was affected by his actions. She wanted to prove to herself and everyone that she did not need him. Since she had repressed her feelings, they were not available to use as she began to relate to another man. Her dependency on her husband had not been acknowledged, and now it came out in her quick involvement with another man.

If we choose to face the ending and deal with it, our minds can be helpful in ferreting out exactly where the ending has occurred in our lives and the nature of the ending. If the mind listens to the emotions and the body, we will know what we are to grieve for and what we need to do in order to grieve.

In griefwork we use our minds to recall both the good things we will miss and the things we will not miss, and also to picture the future. It may require careful thinking to accomplish the external working out of an internal ending. For example, after it became clear to me that I would not spend the rest of my life in that position, I had to think through, as well as feel through and pray through, just what the revelation meant to my life at that time. As I lived further, I had to begin thinking about other possibilities for my life and develop ways to begin to explore them. Each stage of the experience of ending requires careful thinking, in addition to attending to our feelings.

Other people can help us in thinking clearly about what is going on and what our options are. Bouncing ideas off other people can help us think through the ramifications of an ending. We need the best thinking of other people in addition to our own.

A danger lies in turning off our minds so that feelings dominate. In that case we miss what our minds have to teach us. Our feelings, without the help of our minds, may push us to act precipitously or not to act at all. In either case we have not served our best interests in a time of transition.

Paying Attention to Our Spirit. Our spirit is central to any important personal transition. If we are in tune with our spirit, we will be alert to the first intimations of an ending. Our bodies, feelings, and thoughts are used by God's Spirit to communicate with our spirit. As we are sensitive to the messages from the various sources, our spirit can work to discern the *meaning* of the messages and hear God's voice in them.

Discerning God's Call. The realm of the spirit is not governed by the rules of the mind or by scientific principles. Discerning God's call is, therefore, not always an easy matter. The community of faith is crucial in the discernment process. Quakers have had a great deal of experience in the process of discernment, since a central principle of the Religious Society of Friends is that, because Christ is in each of us, we can know Christ's will and Christ can lead and direct our lives. Quakers have devised various means by which individuals can test their leadings. In "clearness committees," selected people meet with a person and, in an atmosphere of worship, attempt to "listen the person into clearness" concerning a decision or dilemma.[8] As Quakers wait in silent worship for a word from God, so we all can wait for clarity concerning our call from God.

Hugh Barbour states that the four major tests that Quakers came to apply to determine if a leading was from God were moral purity, patience, the self-consistency of the spirit, and bringing people into unity. Moral purity has to do with being obedient to God rather than to self-will. Some calls may require sacrifice and may be difficult. We must be patient because our own will is impatient. Most important is self-consistency of the spirit, which is based on the principle that God does not contradict God's self and lead people in conflicting directions. Examples from scriptures and the history of Christianity can also be used as measures of comparison. Finally, a leading from God will bring people into unity, not discord. Where an apparent leading brings discord, members of the community need to examine themselves and their neighbors, in order to test the leading and find the root of the problem.[9]

Including All the Messages. To cut off our minds, our feelings, our spirit, or the messages from our bodies throughout the process of a transition means that we have deprived ourselves of important resources in making the transition. If any one channel dominates and shuts off the others, we miss what the other channels have to tell us. We may seem to sail easily through a transition. The difficulty may come later, when we become depressed or sick or cannot seem to form close relationships. Then we may discover that we have to go back and deal with parts that were earlier denied.

Using Rituals. Endings call for rituals. A crucial element in coping with endings is to ritualize the ending. Our society has devised a variety of ways to ritualize some endings: the school graduation, the bridal shower, the bachelor's party the night before the wedding, the retirement dinner and the gold watch, the celebration in Times Square on New Year's Eve. The need for rituals in faith communities is discussed in chapter 6. In the transient area of northern Virginia, where I lived for a time, one church bids farewell to families who are leaving by presenting them at the end of Sunday morning worship with a banner made by members of the church.

A number of personal endings occur in our lives for which society has no ready-made rituals to help us. In those cases, we will have to find ways to mark the event that fit us and our particular circumstances. For instance, the faculty and staff of the school where I work moved into renovated quarters in a new building. The old building was scheduled to be torn down. One of the faculty invited all interested persons to assemble one morning in the old building and reminisce about the events that had occurred in that space over the years. One man, who had grown up in the house, was able to talk about its initial construction and history before it became school property. The founding dean of the school shared stories about the changing use of the space and some humorous as well as poignant incidents. The occasion served as a marker, a ritual, of an ending.

Especially when internal endings come from deep inside, a ritualistic act can express feelings and attitudes that words cannot describe. For example, the act of taking food to a home where a family member has recently died expresses love and presence in a concrete way. Many rituals before, during, and after the funeral are ways to mark and cope with the ending that has occurred with a death.

In summary, effective coping with an ending requires the

assistance of all of ourselves—feelings, mind, body, and spirit—in the context of community. One or the other may lag behind at a particular point in the process, and we will have to stop and pay special attention to that area. The sense of *chairos*—the right time for an ending to occur—comes to us as we are in tune with God and pay attention to all aspects of our selves.

For Personal Reflection

Think of a recent important transition—or perhaps you are in one right now. Writing in a journal as a way of reflecting on the following questions might be especially useful here. You may also want to share your reflections with a person whom you trust.

How did the ending occur?

When were you first aware of the ending?

How did you proceed to deal with the ending?

Did your body, feelings, mind, and spirit go through it?

Have you finished with most of the ending and said goodbye?

If you haven't, what do you need to do to complete it?

If you don't know how to finish it, are you willing to talk to your minister or a trained counselor for help?

Look at the other peaks—either high or low—on your lifeline (from chapter 2) and the endings involved in each peak.

4

The Second Phase:
The Wilderness

In order to be true to God and to ourselves we must break with the familiar, established and secure norms and go off into the unknown.

—Thomas Merton[1]

Have you ever gotten out of bed in the dark of night in a friend's house? You think you know your way around, so you do not turn on a light. Then you find that objects and furniture are not where you thought they were, and you find yourself disoriented. You feel a moment of panic and stop to catch your breath. Where are you? What's wrong?

Experiencing the Wilderness

We may lose our bearings after we have experienced an internal ending. Consider Marie's story.

Marie had been a research assistant in a large company for a number of years. As a result of a vague sense of dissatisfaction with her position, she thought about ways she could change her assignments so that she once again would feel the challenge and excitement she had initially experienced in that job. After attempting a couple of small changes and discovering that the dissatisfaction did not go away, she realized that she no longer fit that particular job: her time in it had come to an end. She felt relief in putting into words what was going on inside herself, and she could now consider her options.

However, life is strangely different now, as a result of her realization. She sees characteristics about her supervisor that she had not seen before. Even though she is still busy at work and wants to do a good job, she finds herself less personally invested in her performance and the company. She is no longer connected to the role of research assistant. The old ways she used to define herself at work—title, salary, office, responsibilities, respect of co-workers—no longer give her satisfaction. She wonders, If I am not a research assistant here, then who am I? What will I do?

Marie's external appearance and activities may remain the same, but internally her values and perspective are different. The furniture in her heart and mind has been moved around, so that she feels strange, sometimes disoriented.

We may have had experiences similar to Marie's. Like Dorothy in *The Wizard of Oz,* we too can say, "Toto, I don't think we're in Kansas anymore." The question, then, is where are we?

Persons who experience internal endings through no choice of their own may enter into even deeper disorientation. The mother whose child enters kindergarten, the father whose daughter marries, the adolescent who discovers new and strange feelings about the opposite sex are experiencing normal changes that come with living. Each change, however, requires leaving a previous stage and feeling lost and ill at ease for a while before the new stage becomes familiar and comfortable. Likewise, the child who enters the hospital for an appendectomy, the man who loses his leg in a car accident, and the woman who has a mastectomy go through a period of turmoil. The security of who they were—a healthy child, a "normal" man or woman—is now called into question. Feelings of loss, anger, depression, anxiety, and pain may arise. Their lives are permanently altered because of what happened. It takes time to deal with the feelings and adjust to the changes in the body and the self-image. The child may quickly recover and continue with normal activities. The experience of being in a hospital, however—undergoing anesthesia and surgery, recuperating, being related to as sick—will be remembered for the rest of the person's life and will affect the way he or she feels about hospitals and being sick. Obviously the man who loses a leg or the woman who undergoes a mastectomy will never be the same.

The Wilderness Image

After Jesus was baptized, he found himself in a wilderness where he was tested for forty days. During that time he wrestled with questions of personal identity and personal vocation (Matt. 4:1–11; Mark 1:12–13; Luke 4:1–13). This occurred at the time when Jesus was moving into public ministry. His baptism marked the ending of one stage of life and the beginning of a transition, as it can for persons today who are baptized as adults.

The wilderness is a rich metaphor. The people of Israel spent forty years in the wilderness between leaving Egypt and entering the promised land. Elijah went into the wilderness when he was upset with the people of Israel and scared by Jezebel's threats to kill him (1 Kings 19). After Paul's dramatic conversion on the road to Damascus, he spent three days in Damascus without sight and without food and water (Acts 9:9). The wilderness is the place in-between, the place where we are tested, the place where we wrestle with who we are and what we value. In the wilderness we do not have to deal with the normal routines of life, so our unresolved issues stand out clearly.

The wilderness image is used most often in the Old Testament in reference to the forty years that the people of Israel spent between leaving Egypt and arriving in the promised land of Canaan. When the Israelites were later exiled in Babylon, they again saw themselves in a kind of wilderness. In both cases they were a people on the move, awaiting the fulfillment of divine promises. They were being purged of the old and primed for the new.[2]

The concept of wilderness contained a combination of positive and negative meanings for Israel. The word "wilderness" referred to the uncivilized, the edge, the dwelling place of wild creatures and outlaws. During the wilderness wandering, Israel experienced hunger, thirst, snakes, scorpions, and fierce desert nomads.

On the other hand, Israel experienced the care and protection of God as witnessed by the presence of the cloud by day, the fire by night, and the manna God provided for them to eat. It is precisely this combination of positive and negative meanings that is typical of being in-between. It is neither Egypt nor Canaan. "It is outside of civilization, remote, harbouring the sacred both divine and demonic."[3] The wilderness is where we find ourselves after we have left a place, following an ending.

The wilderness contains both a variety and an intensity of feelings. Our wilderness can be a scary and difficult place. The ways we normally define ourselves are no longer available to us. Our role as mother or father has to be redefined when our child leaves home; our involvement at work has to be redefined when the position we have held comes to an end (either internally or externally). Our self-image has to be redefined as we live through many situations: growing older and facing our own mortality, losing a limb or having to adjust to living with a chronic illness or disability, or experiencing positive events such as receiving a job promotion or purchasing a new house. The routines of our existence have been disrupted, and we are thrown into chaos of varying degrees.

A Scary Place. Our particular wilderness is scary because we are not in control. Parts of ourselves that were previously nailed down are now loose and flapping. The secure past is gone, the future is not predictable, and the present is uncomfortable. While we may have been in control in bringing something to an end, we are then thrown into the wilderness, which we did not ask for! For example, if we end a relationship, other events naturally follow. We now have more time on our hands; we are lonely and unsure of where to start to make another close friendship. We also know that a friendship does not happen just because we want it to.

A Difficult Place. Our wilderness is difficult because we feel anxious as a result of being out of control and being unsure of who we are. The anxiety can range from mild to massive, depending on the kind of ending that has occurred, the stage of life we are in, our resources for coping, and our personal history. The anxiety and disorientation can be severe enough that we may begin to wonder if we are going crazy. We may feel as though we have let go of a trapeze bar and are in free flight. We may not be able to see the other bar, although we hope that it will be there at the right moment for us to grab, and the safety net is a long way down! No wonder we feel anxious, afraid, disoriented, and lost.

The way through the wilderness can be treacherous as unresolved issues in our lives burst forth. Matters we thought were settled long ago may present themselves for attention. In any wilderness period we may have to deal with unfinished business from other periods of life. Students often find the college years a middle phase between one part of their life and another. During this time they uncover old griefs and losses and discover parts of themselves that need healing. This is disturbing, until they learn that such self-awareness goes with the territory and, though still painful, can lead to better health.

If you are not consciously aware of having faced a wilderness period in life, do not worry. If you are attentive and open to your internal world, both the normal stages of development and unexpected events and accidents of life will provide ample transitions. Any transition, however small, includes a period of adjustment when we feel off-balance. A small event may provide the symbolic focus for a much more profound shift that has occurred internally as we discussed in the previous chapter.

Reactions to the Wilderness

Given the intensity of the feelings involved in a wilderness experience, we can have a variety of responses. Some of the more common ones follow; you may add others that you have experienced.

Avoidance. Given the nature of the wilderness experience, it is easy to see why we attempt to avoid it. We may deny the wilderness and go on with business as usual. If we are used to being in control, for example, we may be tempted to ignore what is going on internally. Consider George's experience.

George was working on his relationship with his wife, especially on learning to share his feelings and to admit his needs A strong, self-sufficient man, he was attempting to let go of that image and had not yet integrated a new, more whole picture of himself. Then his son began to bring home poor grades from school and to withdraw at home. George attempted to ignore the problems of his son and to keep a façade at work of business as usual. One day a co-worker complained that George was repeatedly late returning from lunch. When George blew his top—a reaction way out of proportion to the incident—he knew something was wrong internally and he had better find out what it might be.

George was attempting to keep his wilderness experience confined to one area of his life, his relationship with his wife. He avoided dealing with the implications of his shift in self-image in the relationships with his son and with his co-workers As George found, such avoidance merely postpones working in those areas and may make the problems more volatile In addition, denying the presence of the wilderness makes us more vulnerable to the stresses of everyday living

Moving Too Quickly. Rather than denying them, we may admit the feelings of confusion and disorientation but want to get through them too quickly and get on with life. Friends and family will give us support for working through our problems, providing we do so efficiently and quickly. For example, it is okay to grieve after a death, or be depressed or upset—*but not for long!* We soon hear from people around us how we ought not dwell on the past but should get out more and forget what happened. If we persist in our grief, we may find ourselves isolated as others withdraw from us. How many times have we heard, or even said, "Sue just needs to get hold of herself" or "Tom is taking this too hard"?

If we take our internal state seriously, we discover that it does not operate on the same schedule as our "instant" culture does. The self needs time for mourning the loss, learning to live with new circumstances, and for healing. This process cannot be rushed. We may go through the motions of getting on with life, but the new beginning has not happened internally. It may be hard to accept the pace given to us in the wilderness.

Moving on too quickly may mean that we have postponed important inner work, work that will arise again in its own time and way. The confusion and disorientation of the wilderness phase can prompt us to examine our values, self-image, and relationship to God and others, as well as our way of saying goodbye. Another failed relationship, another stage in life, another grief comes our way, and we find ourselves crying or thinking about things that happened years ago which still beg to be completed.

Persons who move too quickly to replace a close companion often find it does not work. They discover they cannot be really intimate with, and invested in, the new person until they have finished their grieving over the lost love. The self needs healing in order to be ready to reattach and be vulnerable again to another person. A common reaction on the part of a recently separated or divorced person is to find another person of the other sex with whom to spend time. The need to feel close to someone often leads to a relationship that quickly develops into an intense involvement. The unfinished business of grief, anger, and regret from the old marriage lurks in the background and often ends up sabotaging the new relationship. The need for closeness and affirmation blinds us to warning signals about the other person or about the nature and maturity of the developing relationship.

Retreating to the Past. Another possible reaction to the wilderness is to retreat to the safety of the past, even as the people of Israel wanted to return to the food and fleshpots of Egypt. Even though retreat is not really possible in the case of an accidental transition, we can still pretend! It is not uncommon for a person in counseling to decide that the kind of questioning and struggling necessary for movement into the future is too difficult, so she or he drops out of counseling altogether. How many couples do we know who have been unhappy and as a result split up, only to return to the same unhappy state?

Don had a dream of running his own computer store. He had worked for someone else for years. After finally getting his own store, though, he found that the hours and the responsibility were too much for him. He returned to his old job with an air of resignation.

Young adults in their twenties return home or drop out of college. Faith communities choose pastors who help them live in the past. Retreating to the past is a common reaction—and an understandable one, given the cost of the wilderness period.

Refusing to Budge. A less common reaction is to hunker down in the middle of the wilderness and refuse to move. It's as though we build a tent in the wilderness and settle in for the duration. Some people make the transitional period of adolescence into a style of life that causes them to continue to act and dress as they did as teenagers.

Jose was a man in his twenties who had left home at the height of the Vietnam war without finishing high school. He had traveled across the country many times, never staying in one place for very long. He came in for counseling because he was involved with a woman, as he had been with others in the past, but again could not make up his mind what kind of relationship he wanted with her. It became clear as we talked that he had never settled his identity issues from adolescence; he did not know who he was. Therefore he was unable to be intimate in a committed relationship. He ended up terminating with the woman, terminating with me, and moving on once again.

Bodily Reactions. A wilderness time can be stressful. The body reacts as it does in dealing with any stress: It prepares for fight or flight by releasing certain hormones. Having to control, and in some cases suppress, our natural fight-or-flight reactions puts our body under tension. High blood pressure, ulcers, and rashes are among the many physical problems that appear to be affected, if not triggered, by the tension. It is possible that any organ or system of the body can be affected by stress, since our bodies, emotions, and spirits are interconnected.

Feelings that are denied on a conscious level do not go away. Instead, they remain in our bodies and are expressed in ways that can be detrimental to our physical, emotional, and spiritual health. Anxiety can suppress our immune system, leaving us vulnerable to many physical ailments. The role of anxiety in the health of our bodies is being increasingly recognized so that primary care physicians are now being advised to take time to talk with their patients about their love life, finances, marriage, and feelings.[4]

Spiritual Reactions. I am increasingly convinced that aliveness or deadness of spirit is to a large extent determined by the way in which we move into or refuse to move into certain crucial wilderness times. To refuse to enter the wilderness is to shrink back from life. Each time we refuse, we choose not to heed the call of God into the unknown. We choose to play it safe. In playing it safe, we do not live on the growing edge of abundant life, either with others or with God. As a living organism, we have some choice over whether or not we continue to grow spiritually and psychologically. As a healthy tree has a new ring of growth each year, so we continue to grow. If we stop growing, we become stagnant. Sensitivity to the whispering of God's voice and sensitivity to the needs of self and others begin to die. As the channels of attentive listening and imaginative response cease to be used, they atrophy. As a result, we may die internally at any age, although we may continue to exist for a number of years.

God's Role in the Wilderness

All these reactions, while understandable, do not help us move through the wilderness. As in most areas of life, the way to clear ground on the other side is to go *through* the dark forest. Yet the uncharted region is scary and makes us anxious when we consider plunging ahead.

Valuing Chaos. If we read the Gospel accounts of Jesus in the wilderness, we see that the Spirit of God led Jesus into the wilderness and ministered to him. We may find that the chaotic middle phase is precisely where God speaks most clearly. God appeared to Moses at Sinai while the people of Israel were in the middle of the wilderness. Indeed, the covenant with Israel, which was central to Israel's identity and relationship to God, was given at the midpoint of the wilderness.[5]

Chaos is the primordial condition prior to creativity and is full of energy. "Chaos is not a mess, but rather it is the primal state of pure energy to which the person returns for every true new beginning."[6] As in the original creation story in Genesis 1:1, we may discover that God continues to speak out of chaos and bring order within us. It is crucial to be open to this voice.

Feeling God's Presence. When Jesus was tempted in the wilderness, it is not clear whether or not he felt the presence of God. Luke reports that he was led by the Holy Spirit into the wilderness and that he returned after forty days, in the power of the Spirit (Luke 4:1–2, 14). When the Devil tempted him with scripture, he responded with scripture. However, we can imagine that Jesus might have felt that God was absent at times. He certainly felt forsaken by God on the cross (Mark 15:34). We too may feel that God is absent when we are in the dark middle of transition. When we most need God's presence and comfort, we may find God strangely missing. Our anxiety and aloneness are then heightened.

We need to remember that our feelings do not control the *Amen!* presence or absence of God! When we are in the middle of turmoil and change, our feelings are not an accurate indicator of the reality of God. God is with us whether or not we experience God's presence at any particular moment. Psalm 139 is very clear that there is no place we can go where God is not present. From heaven to hell, from the wings of the morning to the bottom of the sea, God is there. The psalmist reminds us in beautiful birth imagery that God formed us in our mother's womb. The implication is that there is no way that Mother God will abandon her children.

When Jesus is giving the Great Commission to his disciples, before leaving them after the resurrection, he reminds them, "I am with you always" (Matt. 28:20b).

Following God's Leading. God continues to lead by calling us
into the wilderness. God has led us through an ending, as was
discussed in the previous chapter, and we can trust God to
continue to lead us in this wilderness phase. Knowing that God
has led us and continues to go with us, whether or not we
experience God's presence at any particular moment, encourages us to go ahead. Our trust of God, based upon past experience, provides the basis for moving into the chaos of this period.

To follow God's call to move into the wilderness means to pay
attention to it and learn from it. To do that we have to relax our
need for control, to let go our anxiety and allow the wilderness
to happen within us. The wilderness will not kill us, although
we may not be sure about that when we are going through it!

When Our Faith Is in Transition

Our discussion so far assumes that faith remains stable while
other parts of our lives are in transition. However, it is common
for faith to be shaken up when some other parts are coming
apart. When our deepest beliefs are called into question, we are
like a boat bobbing on the ocean, without rudder or anchor.

Importance of Community. A loving community is invalu-
able during this time. Best, of course, is to belong to a community of faith before the crisis occurs. A faith community can be
most supportive if it recognizes and supports the value of questioning and searching in spiritual matters.

During his sophomore year in college, Robert felt the sacred
beliefs he had inherited from his parents beginning to slip
away. He had grown up in a southern town, had attended the
same church as his parents, and had learned a definite way
of looking at the world. Classes in college began to offer a
variety of points of view, so that he was forced to question the
beliefs he had inherited. While sitting in chapel he could sense
the foundations beneath him beginning to sway. Robert's
courses in religion, conversations with close friends, and at-
tendance at discussion groups held at the University Church
gave him some sense of stability and direction during this

in-between time. He ended up changing his major area of study. Years later, he looked back on this period as a very difficult one, but a turning point in the direction of his life.

Isolation is *not* what we need when our faith is shaking. While we need some time alone for personal meditation and self-incubating, we need good friends with whom we can open up and honestly share; friends who will accept us as we are and not judge us. In a community we can find that others are going through a difficult time in their spiritual lives and are supportive of each other. We are also reminded that many have gone through spiritual crises and have survived, and that is a comfort.

Reading and Meditating. For some people, reading the autobiographies of spiritual people can be helpful. Reading some of the great spiritual writers of the past will show us that the "dark night of the soul" is not an uncommon experience.[7] Reading about the struggles of others can encourage us. For example, in the fourth century Augustine struggled with his "life of sin" in his autobiographical *Confessions*[8] and later became one of the most influential leaders of the church. More recently, Harry Emerson Fosdick, well-known writer and preacher at Riverside Baptist Church in New York City during the first half of this century, described in his autobiography[9] the agony of suffering a nervous breakdown and being hospitalized.

Sometimes the affirmations of those who have emerged from the shadows of doubt and struggle can provide a trust fund from which we can borrow until we have "faith funds" of our own. Certain parts of the Bible, such as the psalms that complain to God, the story of Thomas doubting the resurrection of Jesus (John 20:24–29), and the story of Jonah's reluctance to be God's messenger, can be helpful during this time.

Importance of Self-Affirmation. As important and necessary as other people are during this time, in a sense we stand alone in the wilderness, especially when our faith is in flux. We are pushed back onto our own inner resources and our survival skills in the wild place. At those times, we need to remember the following:

I am me and I am acceptable to God.
I do not need to feel guilty for being in this place.
I can and will make it.
I can learn and grow from this experience.
I am thankful to be alive.

Socially Sanctioned Wilderness Times

Certain structures in our society provide the experimentation and time apart that are integral to a wilderness period. We can take advantage of these structures as we work through the middle phase of transitions.

For Adolescents. The teen years are a kind of in-between time—between childhood and adulthood. Adolescents in this country report feeling the chaos and confusion that any wilderness time brings. Erik Erikson has labeled it a "psychosocial moratorium" in which decisions affecting the rest of our lives do not have to be made and there is time for experimenting with different ways of being in the world.[10]

The college years extend the psychosocial moratorium for some students. But when students work and go to college only part-time, or marry while continuing college, the protective shield of the college years is no longer as effective as it once was. The Peace Corps, with its two-year commitment, is another in-between time for people of all ages. For some young people in the 1960s and 1970s, hitchhiking around the country or dropping out of traditional structures became another kind of wilderness experience.

For Adults. Society has recognized the need for a moratorium during adolescence, the transition from childhood to adulthood. It has not recognized and sanctioned the need for such a time during the adult years. However, a moratorium is available for some people. The tradition of the sabbatical in institutions of higher learning, and also now in some elementary and secondary schools, includes some dimensions of such a time. Some corporations now permit an employee to be temporarily reassigned to a public service project. An overseas assignment is another way that some people find "time out" from their usual routines. An increasing number of middle-aged and older adults are returning to college and graduate school for further education, for a time of reflection and reevaluation. Retreat centers around the country provide another context for reflection. With the recent popularization of the crisis of mid-life, some people have taken time off after leaving one job before jumping into another one. They may do something very different for a while before returning to their career pattern, while others may make a switch in basic direction. Perhaps someday periods of moratorium throughout life will become more accepted and supported.

Attitudes for the Journey

Our mind-set makes a difference in the relative ease or difficulty with which we go through the wilderness phase. The following attitudes can aid us in traversing the uncertain terrain.

Faith That We Will Come Through. Perhaps the most important attitude during the wilderness time is a basic faith that we will come through. We can look back at earlier times when we came through. God, who has been with us in other important times in our lives, will not fail us now. As God says to Isaiah, "I will make a way in the wilderness and rivers in the desert" (43:19b, RSV). Both the necessary trust and the possible danger are reflected in a whimsical way in Martha Courtot's poem "Crossing a Creek":

> crossing a creek
> requires 3 things:
> a certain serenity of mind
> bare feet
> and a sure trust
> that the snake we know
> slides silently
> underwater
> just beyond our vision
> will choose to ignore
> the flesh

> that cuts through
> its territory
> and we *will* pass through
> some people think crossing a creek
> is easy
> but i say this—
> all crossings are hard
> whether creeks, mountains
> or into other lives
>
> and we must always believe
> in the snakes at our feet
> just out of our vision
> and we must practice believing
> we *will* come through[11]

The poem is correct: All crossings are hard. That is reality, and that is where we all begin in times of transition. Equally important and correct, however, is our conviction that we will come through.

God Is Present. In addition to faith, the other helpful spiritual stance is our belief that God is in the wilderness, as well as having led us there. God's presence in the wilderness means that there is something important for us in the wilderness. God makes possible for the trip the useful mind-sets of curiosity, an attitude of exploration, and attentive listening.

God's presence may not be constantly obvious during the wilderness phase. As I said earlier, our faith may be shaken at the same time. However, beneath the turmoil and confusion lies the solid bottom which God provides. Many spiritually sensitive people report feeling that God was present during this chaotic phase as the ground under their feet or the bottom to their well. God is present in the love and care of others, in the sequence in which events occur, in the small voice inside, in the place of quiet in the midst of chaos.

If we feel the presence of God, then we are able to relax and focus on what we need to learn and do in the wilderness. While parts of the phase may not be pleasant, we can know that the trip is important and our learning will be great. In fact, this trip can be the most important one in our life.

Uncertainty Can Be Valuable. Because this second movement in transitions—going through the wilderness—involves living with basic uncertainty, it is important for us to have an appreciation of the value of such uncertainty. While we all need some things nailed down and secure, we can discover that uncertainty also provides the leaven for life. Even for people who plan their vacations ahead of time, some of the most memorable events occur when something unscheduled happens. A recent trip on a familiar road, for example, brought me to a detour. In traveling the back road, I found some beautiful country I would never have enjoyed otherwise.

Some people find that absolute certainty is closer to death than to life. One writer states that "without the nourishment provided by the ability to rest in uncertainties, mysteries, and doubts, the soul begins to starve."[12] Uncertainty may force us to ask questions and look at life in a different way. This affirmation of uncertainty will help us acknowledge the value of wilderness journeys and give these times the space they require in our lives.

Many people find that the wilderness experience provides an aliveness and a positive, yeasty ferment that is in sharp contrast to the deadness often felt before entering this phase. The pain and confusion of this time is offset by the exhilaration of living and struggling in a vital life process. Participating in this universal human experience provides a connection with all other human beings.

Creativity and Growth Are Toward the Unknown. Finally, our journey through the wilderness will be aided by a basic awareness that creativity and growth are always toward what is unknown. To go over the known involves repetition, which can be helpful in reinforcing what we have learned. If that is all we do in our lives, however, we live a structured life that contains little challenge. To move into the unknown is risky and requires a willingness to be vulnerable. However, the reward is flexibility and openness to hearing a fresh word from God.

Becoming vulnerable and moving into the unknown also taps the wellspring of creativity deep within. By moving into a place where everything is not nailed down, our creative potential has an opportunity to play and suggest possibilities. New energy is released for the journey.[13]

With these basic attitudes, we can value the wilderness and use it as a positive resource. The wilderness can become a place to which we retreat regularly, even daily, for renewal and sustenance. Quiet solitude and meditation—which can include deep inner struggle and honest wrestling—are always available as channels through which we can enter that wilderness. As the desert hermits in the early Christian era discovered, we can see more clearly in the wilderness. When a major transition occurs and we enter into a wilderness zone, we can be more comfortable with the terrain and less afraid of going through it if we know that creativity and growth are possibilities.

Helps Along the Way

Once we have entered the wilderness through the leadership of God, and with the right attitude, the following suggestions may be helpful.

Pay Attention. The most important thing is to pay attention. Listen carefully to what is happening in terms of feelings, needs, and unfinished issues. To do this, we may need to cultivate a "third ear" that listens to our insides. Many persons in our culture, especially men, do not know how to pay attention to themselves. We can learn. It requires that we focus inwardly rather than outwardly.

When we begin to pay attention, we may find that feelings of confusion and anxiety are common. We certainly do not like being in that situation, and may complain and lament. The people of Israel did their share of complaining in the wilderness (Ex. 15:24; 16:2–3; 17:3). Even as Israel did, we may regress and feel like children whom God, or some parent, ought to rescue. We will feel so needy at times during our wilderness journey that nothing and no one can possibly meet all our needs. We may need a place of comfort and security for retreat. Paying attention will alert us to what we need at any particular moment.

Allow Time and Unstructured Space. If we move to activities too quickly, we become performance-oriented and lose the wilderness meaning for ourselves. There is no cookbook recipe that is guaranteed to get us to firm ground. One friend recently wrote to me the following:

> *The essence of my wilderness journey at the moment is this: putting myself into a state of long-term intentionality. The best way I can say it is this: the journey is* into a state of being. . . . *Don't know if that's clear. It was hard to find words for this important insight.*

The letter went on to explain that "long-term intentionality" meant giving this transition all the time that it required and being intentional about letting go of some structure and control so that the author of this letter could just be.

This kind of work takes time and energy, and we give ourselves a great gift when we can allow the work to proceed. We can find what helps us do that work. We will know how long to remain in the wilderness, if we pay attention to ourselves and to God's Spirit as it speaks to our spirit.

Maintain Certain Routines. The other side of allowing time and unstructured space is maintaining selected personal routines so that some structure is provided. Routines of eating, sleeping, and exercise are important. If everything is in turmoil, the resulting chaos can be too much to handle. As part of our spiritual discipline, we may want to fast or stay up all night in prayer and meditation. Jesus fasted in the wilderness, and Paul fasted after his Damascus experience. Even in doing that, however, we need to maintain some routines. In combining the essence of these first two suggestions, we should stay occupied but not busy.

Give Yourself Permission to Experiment. Now that we are breaking free from former roles and bonds, experimentation is possible in ways that may not have been available to us since our adolescent years. We need to take advantage of the time. In the chaos, we can think new thoughts, try new things, go to new places. Some of it can be for fun and recreation. However, if we attempt these new things while remaining open to God's leading, the experimenting will help us find a way through the wilderness.

One woman, recently separated from her husband, felt the need to go camping by herself in a large national forest. She had never done that before. It was scary for her, but she went. Upon returning, she reported a new sense of self-security and independence she had never felt before.

The early years of widowhood can be an important time for experimentation and adjustment. New possibilities can be explored and old, untried dreams lived out. New sides of ourselves can be developed which our spouse had earlier fulfilled.

One widow was sharing how busy she was, attending meetings and driving places. Her husband, who had died a year earlier, did not like her to drive. She was now enjoying driving and meeting other people.

A man in his late seventies who lost his wife began to try his hand at cooking, including finding new recipes and buying the groceries. It took time to become accustomed to preparing three meals a day, but he found a routine and is proud of his newly developed ability.

Going to the beach or the mountains during the wilderness time can be healing for some persons. In traveling to a particular place we can also play out a recurring dream. One couple, after each had graduated from professional schools and before they settled down into careers, chose to take a trip around the world for six months. We need to ask ourselves, What are the yearnings inside? Remember when we said, "If I ever had time I would like to do that?" Now may be the time.

Be Gentle with Yourself. Because of the time, energy, and struggle involved in transitions, we need to let up on self-demands. Do not push; it is okay if you become more forgetful or need more sleep or feel mentally dull. Any time that we undergo significant stress, we need to be gentle with ourselves. The wilderness experience is one of those important times. For persons with high self-expectations, being gentle on themselves can be especially hard to do.

Keep Communication Open. Keep open a communication line to the outside world. We can get lost in the unfamiliar terrain! At least one other person should know what is going on with us and where we are in our pilgrimage through the wilderness. An experienced pastor, mature friend or family member, spiritual guide, pastoral counselor, or therapist could be that communication link for us. That person can be helpful for feedback, support, accountability, and learning.

Keep a Journal. Keep a journal of what is occurring inside you. Many people find writing to be helpful in clarifying what is going on internally, in probing further, and in recording thoughts and feelings for later reflection. In order to make the writing personal and reflective of what is happening to us internally, we will have to write differently from the way we were taught in school. Do not be concerned about grammar, spelling, sentence structure, or neatness. The aim is to put into words what is being revealed to us. We may want to try writing with our less dominant hand, or writing diagonally across the page, or using a brightly colored pen—anything to break the old patterns from school and to access our intuitive process.

Pay Attention to Dreams. Paying attention to dreams is one of the best ways to live creatively through all the phases, but especially through the wilderness time. Recording them in a journal for later reflection is helpful. Our dreams are our potential friends, if we spend time with them. They can give us important data of which we may not be aware. We are the ones best able to make sense of our own dreams. Sharing them with another trusted person, however, may give us some additional information as that person shares what the dream might mean.[14] The value of dreams is shown in Jay's experience.

After years of work, Jay was about to receive his Ph.D. degree. He dreamed that the old organ in the church in which he grew up was receiving major renovation, including large new pipes. When he awoke, he became aware that the degree was making him feel larger and more resonant, like pipes on an organ. Receiving the degree was obviously changing the way he looked at himself. Listening to his dream made Jay understand the significance of this internal shift.

Wait on God. Waiting on God is the foundation for all the previous suggestions. The wilderness is a time of waiting and listening for the Spirit of God in our lives. Whatever disciplines help us to wait can be useful: prayer, meditation, scripture reading, fasting, spiritual retreat, a spiritual guide or friend, physical exercise. We are attempting to stay centered in God as we go through this middle phase of transition. In staying centered, we are most open to hearing God's word for us.

Waiting in the midst of chaos may be the hardest thing that we ever do. The natural inclination for many of us is to *do* something—anything! Our anxiety demands an outlet in activity. Doing anything seems better than just sitting. However, waiting is what is often called for—looking for signs and portents on the horizon, to be sure, but still waiting. "Don't just do something. Stand there!" may be our best motto. Just be.

The waiting needs to be an expectant waiting, much like waiting for childbirth. We are to watch while we wait. The waiting is hope-full. After jumping up and down from anxiety, we may need to ask God for the patience for watchful waiting. We will discuss this further in the next chapter.

The guiding light for all these suggestions is to pay attention to ourselves as resting in the hands of God and find out what fits for us at this time and place in our life. We will find what fits if we give ourselves permission to experiment and not expect instant results. The following case is a good example.

Ned came to counseling because he did not know if he wanted to stay married. Although a respected member of the community, a regular church attender, and a seemingly ideal family man, he was not sure if he liked being any of those things. They no longer satisfied him, but he did not know what he wanted. He ended up leaving his wife and moving into a hovel, because he felt guilty about leaving.

He began to take an honest look at himself. He realized that he had always lived to make other people happy, so that he did not know who *he* was or what *he* wanted. Ned was an identical twin, so that he was seen from the beginning as part of a twosome. He did well in his job, which involved negotiating disputes. He usually related to people by tuning in to what they needed and then giving it to them. He tended to collect dependent, needy people, especially women, around him.

Ned left the security of his marriage and an accepted place in the community but has not yet arrived at a comfortable new place. He is in between and feeling anxious and off-center. For the first time in his life he is taking a hard look at himself, and that is not easy.

He is dealing with this time by paying attention to himself, by searching inside to see what he can find. Ned was afraid there would be nothing in the center, but now he knows differently. Suffering from low self-esteem, he finds it almost impossible to know what he wants and difficult to give himself anything. However, he is doing two good things for himself every day: running, which he describes as the most peaceful time of the day, and sitting in the park and contemplating. He has lost weight, which he feels good about. He is paying attention to his dreams, although he remembers few of them. Ned is attending another church and is finding the presence of God a comfort to him.

At first he wanted instant change. Now Ned is beginning to sense that it took him a long time to become the way he is, and it is going to take time to move through this period of wilderness.

In using some of these helps during the wilderness phase, we can find this to be one of the most alive, creative times in our lives. Painful and confusing though it is, we know that we are actively involved in a process moving toward rebirth, as God calls us to a new place.

For Personal Reflection

Continue with the same transition that you thought about at the end of the last chapter. Did you experience a wilderness time during that transition?

If you did, did you recognize it and let yourself enter into it?

Did you allow enough time and space in your life for it?

What was it like for you?

Who was your link outside the wilderness, if you had one?

What did you learn from it?

How did you experience God?

Are you in a time of wilderness right now?

If so, what are you doing to cope with it and make good use of it?

Are there other things you could be doing to make this a productive time?

5

The Third Phase:
Beginnings

Behold, I am doing a new thing;
* now it springs forth, do you not perceive it?*
I will make a way in the wilderness
* and rivers in the desert.*
                              —Isaiah 43:19, RSV

In one sense we are always beginning anew. Each day, each hour, each minute is different from any other time in our lives, with challenges and opportunities in some ways unlike any others. We have never lived this particular moment before and never will again, given this specific context and our own history and future. This moment is unrepeatable; that fact makes us a beginner. No other person or book can tell us how to live this moment because it has never been lived before, in all its particularity and uniqueness. Life becomes a boring treadmill when we focus on the sameness, rather than the uniqueness, of the moments of our lives.

Out of Our Control

In a significant personal transition, an internal beginning occurs only after we have been through both an ending and the wilderness. Unlike endings and the wilderness, beginnings happen in their own good time. In some instances we have a choice whether to end some relationship or commitment; we may choose how to deal with the ending once it has happened.

In terms of the second phase, we can choose whether to

enter the wilderness and what to do once we are there. However, internal beginnings are different in that we have *no* choice over when the beginning happens. We can move on to an external beginning and find a new spouse or new job, for example. The internal beginning, however, may not occur at the same time as the external beginning. Most of us like to feel in control of our lives, so that waiting for a beginning to occur is not comfortable. We would like to be able to make it happen when *we* are ready.

Living on the boundary between the wilderness and a new beginning may be the most difficult place of all. Really working on the chaos may create the feeling that there is little left for us to do, yet the internal beginning has not yet appeared. Whereas we are thrown into chaos after an ending, a beginning happens more subtly.

Beginning as a Birth

A beginning is similar to the birth of a baby. Conception is easier to prevent than to make happen. At the moment of conception, the mystery of new life occurs. It is a process as old as humankind, yet still not completely understood. The new beginning is deep inside the mother and not obvious to anyone at first, not even the mother.

If this is the first conception for both the woman and the man, their identities are now forever changed to include being a mother and father. Their carefree days are ended for the time being. Their self-images have changed, as well as the way they are perceived by others. The new beginning does not become real and concrete until nine months later. In the intervening time, the fetus grows and develops, dependent on the mother for nourishment and the right environment, but strangely independent in terms of gender and growth governed by an orderly pattern that is laid down in its genes.

As do all beginnings, the actual birth occurs in its own good time. The infant comes when it is ready. The mother works hard, in order to prepare the way and help it happen, but she cannot make it happen at a certain time or determine the nature of the outcome.

When the infant emerges from the mother, there is a moment of reverent suspense: Will the infant begin to breathe on its own and thereby begin to take on responsibility for its own life? If the infant does, we rejoice and give thanks to God, aware that the birth has happened through us but not totally because of us.

A new beginning is in many ways like the birth process. The beginning may have been growing inside us for a long time before we become aware of it. We can do some things that help to make a beginning happen. Like a baby, our beginning emerges in its own good time, even though we work hard to facilitate its arrival. When the beginning occurs, we give thanks to God.

Not a single birth is recorded during the forty years that Israel was in the wilderness! Given the fertility of the people of Israel when they were in Egypt, this absence is even more striking. A whole generation dies in the wilderness. Then when the Israelites cross the Jordan River, circumcisions occur and the natural life cycle resumes.[1] The wilderness is a time for incubation and brooding, as a hen sits on her eggs. The time apart from life interrupts the natural cycle of life. The natural cycle resumed when the Israelites were led by God into the land of Canaan, where a new beginning was made.

Kinds of Beginnings

There are external and internal beginnings. Each will be considered separately.

External Beginnings. External beginnings are usually in our control. We decide whether to take a new job, or begin a new relationship, or buy another house. Even when an ending occurs that we did not choose, we are still in control of our response. We can even ignore the chaotic middle phase and quickly move on to something else, an external beginning, if we want to.

There may be a time lag between the external and the internal beginning. In many cases the external beginning occurs some time before the internal beginning occurs. An external beginning can happen quickly. However, an external beginning can call up unfinished business of which we were not at first aware. This area will have to be tended to before the internal beginning will occur. For example, in beginning a new job we may discover some unresolved issue in relation to our previous position. Relationships with persons at the previous job may not feel completed; long-standing grievances may continue to nag us; feelings of inadequacy at the other job may show up in the present position as insecurity in learning the new responsibilities. Even though we may have decided to leave the other job only after careful thought and planning, we still may find that the transition process is not completed after we have made the change. A friend had the habit of returning to his previous place of employment several weeks after he had left and walking around the area after hours. In his mind he had imaginary conversations with persons there, recalled experiences he had while working there, and concluded by saying goodbye.

Internal Beginnings. A true internal beginning takes time. The beginning anew may be much slower if the transition occurred as the result of a trauma. In that situation, there are more feelings to work through and adjustments to make. Even in normal life-stage changes, Daniel Levinson found in his research with men that about five years lapsed between the breakup of one stage of life and the beginning of another.[2] In the following case, Jane found that it took a long time to move on to a new beginning after the death of a parent.

Jane has felt rootless ever since her father, her last parent, died over five years ago. Two years ago, after a time of wrestling with herself and with her vocation, she experienced a powerful Christian conversion. About a year later she felt led to attend a theological school to develop her gifts in a Christian framework and to deepen her newfound spiritual life. To assist in spiritual exploration and development she has regular meetings with a person who serves as her spiritual guide. Recently she has been going alone on spiritual retreats for more intense, focused times of looking at her relationship with God. After returning from a recent spiritual retreat, she writes:

> *Suddenly, truly, my own existence: standing on my own two feet (with some outside help to be sure), with God as the platform/ground. I've been floating around in adolescence/ orphanhood since my father died; now it feels as though I have found myself as an adult. It feels like the effective end of the 5½ year period of transition since my father died.*

With her father's death, Jane clearly experienced an ending. She was thrown into the wilderness for over five years. She worked hard during that time, to pay attention to what was happening internally and to learn from the wilderness. The real internal beginning is now occurring.

Overlapping of Phases

Our lived experience of these movements or phases reveals that overlapping occurs. The ending itself is something new in our lives. In that way it has some characteristics of being a beginning. Elements of unresolved grief from the ending need to be dealt with during the wilderness and even into the new beginning. The griefwork gets knitted together piece by piece, so that in the middle of a new beginning we may discover another aspect of the ending yet to be finished. Even though the beginning may be a happy one that we choose, we may still have to deal with some sadness.

Likewise, there will be times after an internal beginning has started that we will feel thrown back into chaos and will wonder if any progress has been made. Such relapses may discourage us unless we remember that it is normal to go back and forth between phases. Given this overlap, the general flow during a transition is from an ending, through a chaotic middle phase, into beginning anew.

Blocks to New Beginnings

There may be times when we watch, pray, and listen, and the new beginning never seems to happen. We do not know how long is long enough to wait. For most of us, any length of time will seem too long. A review of the previous stages may reveal that we did the personal work but still feel blocked and stuck. Following are some possible causes for the blockage.

Hesitance. We may not be proceeding with a beginning because we are hesitant about it. This hesitation in moving into a new beginning is portrayed well in Martha Courtot's poem "Thaw":

> No matter how long the Winter is
> Thaw comes
> season by season
> we learn this
> too slowly
>
> No matter how long we have spent
> wrapped in a frozen season
> no matter how deep under the snow
> the private grief lies
> one day . . .
>
> thaw comes
>
> we are never prepared for it
>
> and what was once safe for our feet
> changes
> water released from ice and mud and madness
> and we open our eyes to
> earth-shift, stone-change
>
> everything thawing
> thawing like a madness
> the earth opening
> water running
>
> and all of our secrets
> exposed.[3]

As this poem points out so nicely, we *say* we want the thaw and we *think* we want the thaw, after the long winter. However, when the thaw comes, we are not prepared for it. No matter how self-aware we are or how well we have gone through the previous phases, we do not know what the beginning will be like. We cannot prepare for it and we cannot control when or how it happens, so we are caught off guard. As a result we feel hesitant about the beginning.

Jill felt that her time with her current job was at an end. She had been there for over ten years, was competent at what she did, but had begun to feel stale. After looking at different possibilities within the company, she felt it was time to do something else. She did not know in what direction to move next. She wrote some letters, made some inquiries, talked to friends, and prayed about it. However, nothing seemed to fit her just right. Then one day, after two years of searching, it suddenly occurred to her that working in a public service organization would pull together all that she felt she wanted to do at this stage in her life. She wondered why it had not occurred to her before. Her husband and teenage son said they had already told her she was cut out for such a position, but she had not been ready to hear it. She was surprised!

What was once safe, changes. Even though we may not like the place or job or relationship we are in, it has become familiar. There is comfort and safety, if not joy, in familiarity. Jill's previous job was secure for her. She did it well, made a good salary, and was liked by her colleagues. Now that was going to change.

A beginning can feel like madness, where things are not as they seem. Martha Courtot uses the word "madness" twice in her poem. While entering wilderness can be like an entry into madness after we let go of our old world, entry into a beginning can also be like an entry into madness.

Jill wondered if she was crazy to think about changing fields. She was forty-five years old and had no experience in public service organizations. Her first inquiries made it clear that there were more applicants than needed for such organizations. Her son would soon be entering college, while she was considering taking a significant salary cut. Jill's father, who grew up in the Depression, said she must be crazy! Yet Jill felt pulled; it was her calling.

Our secrets are exposed. A beginning makes us vulnerable in a way that nothing else can do. Like a newborn infant, we feel fragile and strange when thrust into a new environment. In this new environment, we may feel inept at what others do with ease. A beginning makes us come out of the woodwork and declare ourselves, so that we are more public, more exposed.

Jill got a job working with United Way. While she had felt very comfortable and competent in her previous job, she now felt awkward, like a beginner, which she was. She had to admit that she could not do some things; she had to ask for help from colleagues and friends, and she had to scramble to catch up. She sometimes felt as though her human frailties were hung out for everyone to see.

Dependence. Most of us are more dependent than we are willing to admit: dependent on others, on our daily routines, on the different roles we play, on our jobs. One writer talks about the way in which our society encourages various addictions, of which co-dependence is one manifestation. The primary characteristic of a co-dependent person is relying on others for meaning and a sense of self. In extreme cases, co-dependents use relationships like alcoholics use alcohol.[4]

Striking out on our own is difficult if we are co-dependent persons. Such launching out means we must make our own decisions and set the course for our own lives. That is just what we as co-dependent persons have trouble with.

Living in the wilderness does have certain benefits. We may have less responsibility and fewer commitments, while getting more attention and care from our friends than we did before. A fresh beginning can mean a loss of some support structures, perhaps even the disapproval of some friends and family. Continuing to work in an office where the boss is a tyrant may provide closeness with other employees who feel the same way. A common enemy can pull us together. What would we do without these people, and the income, and the structure?

Fear of Success. If we have low self-esteem, we may feel we are not worthy to succeed. Success would prove us wrong, would prove that we *are* a person of worth and dignity. A new beginning might move us in the direction of success, so we'd better find ways to stay lost in the wilderness. If we do come out and begin afresh, we can usually find some way to muck it up and turn it into a failure.

While we may smile as we read the above lines, underneath the smile is a deep recognition that we have trouble allowing ourselves to succeed.

Another reason for the fear of success is that we may outdistance our parents. Doing better than our parents, while often touted in the American dream, forces us to change our self-image. If our parents are secretly competitive with us, it can make success even more difficult to allow and enjoy.

Fear of Failure. If the fear of success does not get us, the fear of failure will! Our country and our economy are built on success. Add to this a childhood in an achievement-oriented family, and we can easily emerge as hard-working persons with high standards. There is nothing wrong with being hard-working except when the underside is the inability to relax and have fun—and a fear of failure. Failure, for many of us, is the ultimate taboo. "Because of the special emphasis we place on success, America is the cruelest country in which to fail."[5]

Precisely because we cannot control a beginning, we cannot know ahead of time whether it will lead to success or to failure. We are taking a risk; we might fall on our face. And that is our fear.

Up to this point, we have been talking about success and failure as defined by society and family. Following God's leading into a transition means following another standard than the one usually used in our society. Experiencing an ending and going through the wilderness time results in a beginning whose success is measured more by internal criteria than by the external standards of culture. Therefore, what others may see as not successful for us, we may see as being very satisfying and even transformative.

A False Start. Sometimes we jump so quickly into a new chapter of our lives that we do not finish the previous chapters. The price we pay is that the new chapter proves not to work. The new marriage goes sour after a few months or years; the new job, which seemed so exciting at first, soon proves to be a disaster; the move from the city back to the country at first looked idyllic but now feels isolated. When a false start occurs, the sooner we can admit it the better. The problem often lies in the fact that we have a lot of ego invested in making it work, especially in the face of earlier advice that such a drastic change was too much, or too soon, or would never work. Our stubbornness can cause us to keep our head in the sand, not allowing us to face facts or begin to take corrective action. We eventually discover that denying our failure does not make it go away. Tragedy occurs when we admit our failure so late in life that we feel it is too late to do anything about it.

It is never too late to do something about it! No matter what our age or what our circumstances, we *can* do something. The first thing is to admit we made a mistake, and the sooner the better. The second thing is to talk to a trusted friend or skilled person and explore the options. It is foolish to make a second mistake by suddenly making another major move that may not work. We need to return to the middle phase of chaos and experimentation. In actuality we never left that stage internally. We are now simply acknowledging that fact and paying attention to where we really are. We need to back up and do some more internal work. In order to do this, assistance from competent people is very important, almost essential.

Unfinished Business. The remaining possibility is that some unfinished business from our past is blocking our path into the next phase. Unresolved hurt, anger, and fear from earlier relationships may be preventing our moving ahead.

Alice was going through the transition of having a daughter who was a teenager. She came for counseling because she found herself becoming angry when her husband hugged their daughter, and she could not understand why she felt that way. After some exploration of her feelings and her past, she recovered the memory that she had been molested by her father when she was in her early teens. In talking through her feelings about her father and the molestation, she began to separate that incident from the times when her husband hugged her daughter. Then she was more able to adjust to being the mother of an adolescent.

As Alice found out, incidents that have been long forgotten can still carry emotional baggage that weighs us down. Especially during times of transition, this emotional baggage seems to come out of the closet to trip us up. We may not even recall the incidents until we begin to focus on the past and pull on the slender cords that connect us to our history.

We may have unfinished business around transitions that we experienced earlier in our lives but went through poorly. They may weigh on us now and prevent us from proceeding with our journey. We may feel regret and guilt about them. We would do them differently if we could do them over. After reading this book, you may feel that you wish you knew these things years earlier! In order to sort through our attic and see what we want to keep and what we want to get rid of, we might find it helpful to talk to a trained person.

A Beginning Not Recognized or Accepted. Real tragedy occurs when a beginning happens inside us and we either do not recognize it or cannot allow ourselves to accept it. If we are not watching and praying, it is possible not to see the beginning. Life goes on as usual. For most of the people in Bethlehem, the night of Jesus' birth was like every other night of the year. Even the innkeeper, who allowed Mary and Joseph to spend the night in the shed or cave with the animals, had no idea of the new beginning that was occurring in his own stable! If a hired hand from the inn came out to feed the animals and saw the newborn baby, would he have noticed anything unusual? For the shepherds who came, however, it was a beginning that changed the rest of their lives.

Even if we do not recognize it, the beginning can take root and grow and flourish to the point where it commands our attention. A number of men have no idea when puberty began in them. Their voices deepened, bodies grew and matured, and hormones began to secrete. Only later did they become aware of an interest in the other sex and dating.

The danger, of course, is that the new beginning may be stifled and snuffed out through either inattention or being trampled underfoot. For females just beginning to menstruate, a trauma can alter the monthly cycle or prevent it from occurring for months or even years. However, there is a kind of biological pressure that makes it return—unlike other personal beginnings.

Especially in this country, spiritual stirrings in a person's soul may be ignored or stifled because we do not know what to do with them and they may make us feel ridiculous. We may be afraid that we will be like the evangelists we see on television, or whatever kind of religionist who turns us off. We may not have a language to express the spiritual awakening that is trying to happen inside us. So we ignore or stifle spiritual impulses to reach out in prayer to God or to speak about the state of our soul.

We may also refuse to accept a new beginning because we have such low self-esteem. When we feel bad enough about ourselves, we will have difficulty seeing a new possibility coming to birth inside us. Because of lack of hope, we do not allow ourselves to see the birth of hope; because of lack of self-esteem, we cannot imagine that anything good or new could really happen to us; because of depression, we turn our backs to the light and end up standing in the darkness of our own shadow; because of feeling bad for so long, we may be afraid of the changes that would occur if we admitted the new, good feeling into our lives.

Helps Along the Way

The distinctive nature of a beginning requires particular ways of responding. Following are some guidelines you may find useful.

Listen. Of primary importance is continuing to listen to the call of God's Spirit. God has led us out of a secure place and into the wilderness. God will not abandon us there but will lead us into a new place, even as the Israelites were led finally to the promised land. Once we have made an external beginning, it is easy to assume that the process is now complete; we can thank

God and move on. However, the internal beginning has to be tended to just as carefully as we tended to the ending and the middle phase.

The Spirit may be speaking to us through our own yearnings, groans, curiosity, and joys. God, who was incarnated in Jesus, may be speaking in a very incarnational way through our bodies and feelings. Our bodies, through the change in energy level and health of the different systems, will clue us in to whether or not our present state is a good one. In paying attention to the flow of energy in the different parts of our day, we might begin to get clues as to what works well for us and what does not. If our bodies feel energized after volunteering time at the local day-care center, even though we are in the middle of a wilderness, we need to remember that as we consider future directions. If we wake up in the morning with a sense of aliveness and well-being that has not been generally true during the wilderness time, a beginning may be occurring. God may be using our body to communicate with us.

We need also to listen to our feelings. Our joy, sadness, un-happiness, regret, anger, fear, and pain will give us important information about the nature of the phase in which we are currently living. If it becomes increasingly difficult to be de-pressed, we may be on the threshold of a new beginning.

Yearnings and fantasies that flit through our minds are espe-cially important in attempting to hear the call of God to a new beginning. We tend to ignore, or not even be aware of, our yearnings.

> Already in your past life from time to time, God ... has whispered into your heart just that very wonderful thing, whatever it is, that [God] is wishing you to be, and to do, and to have. And that wonderful thing is nothing less than what is called *Your Heart's Desire.* Nothing less than that.[6]

It is easy to pass off our heart's desire, our yearnings, either as selfish or as the creation of an idle mind. It *may* be, but it also may be the voice of God. Brutal honesty with ourselves, prayer, and frank discussion with others can aid us in discerning the origin of such yearnings. The section in chapter 3 on discern-ment also applies here.

Watch and Pray. To watch and pray is what Jesus asked his disciples to do while he went farther into the Garden of Gethsemane (Matt. 26:41). The early church was often admonished to watch and pray while waiting for the Lord to return (e.g., 2 Peter 3:12–13). To watch and pray remains good advice. To watch means that we are hopeful and expectant. To pray keeps us centered in the Spirit of God while we are waiting. Our anxiety about not knowing when and how the beginning will come can be gathered up and given to God in prayer. Our need to control can likewise be turned over to God, so that we let God be God in our lives. While we cannot make a new beginning happen, we can be open to its occurring and alert to seeing it when it does occur. We can place ourselves in a position of receptivity. That requires keeping vigil.

In the report on her experience during a spiritual retreat mentioned earlier in this chapter, Jane goes on to say:

> *There's an enormous sense of needing/desiring to stay awake, to keep vigil. I thought quite a bit about this surprising thing. Keeping vigil over something new inside me. Gestation. . . . I walk alongside, or have within me, a new part of me that I get to be with (what fun!), even though I can't see it clearly yet. . . . The knights of the Middle Ages would keep vigil in the chapel all night before going into a holy battle like the Crusades; it was a kind of ritual, sanctifying thing: a dedication to a cause, to God.*

Watching and praying does not mean that we are waiting to be rescued. Watching means an alertness to an internal movement that signals God's quiet leading to the next phase. We are still responsible to do the work and make the decisions. In a rescue fantasy, the responsibility is taken out of our hands, while something or someone from the outside comes in and delivers us.

Watching and praying does not mean shutting our eyes to what is going on. While it involves quietness and withdrawal, it does not mean denial. In fact, watching and praying can provide a special sensitivity to the environment, which we may not have when we are busy and running.

Explore. While we listen, watch, and pray, we can also do some tentative exploring of new internal beginnings. We can play with the idea of what it would be like to give up our misgivings and struggles and allow a new beginning to happen. What would that feel and be like? What if it happened right now? We can make forays with our imagination into different possibilities for new beginnings. In our exploration, we may discover that one possibility begins to take root and grow.

While listening to God and our innermost being, we can try taking a step in one direction and experience what that is like. As we step back to where we originally started, we can reflect on the step we took and attempt to discern whether that seems to be the direction in which we are called to go. Asking God to give us light for the next step is a good prayer to use daily. If we pray such a prayer, then we need actually to take a step and see what happens. Consider Elizabeth:

> Elizabeth appeared to be stuck in the wilderness phase. She wanted desperately to get on with her life and find a new beginning, but nothing she tried in her personal growth, her living arrangements, or her job seemed to work out. While she continued to work on issues from her past, she began to read the classified section of the local paper every day, especially the ads for jobs and for housing. When she came upon one that seemed interesting, she would imagine herself in that job or in that housing arrangement and what it might be like for her. She later went to interview for several different kinds of jobs in order to get a better feel of what they would be like.
>
> In addition, Elizabeth began to consider different types of living arrangements. She would make inquiries, then come back and think about how the arrangements fitted her and talk them over with friends. All the while her constant prayer was that God would show her the way.

Be Playful. Watching, waiting, and praying does not mean we have to be dour! Even here, playfulness is appropriate and helpful. A playful lightness will cushion our failures and prevent our pushing too hard on any one option when it is not right for us. Humor may be one of God's gifts to us during times of transition. Have you known some people who experience a traumatic change in life and are able to laugh at parts of it? One woman was going in for cancer surgery. Her surgeon came into her room to speak to her the morning of the operation, pulled down the sheet from over her head, and saw a Halloween mask facing him! Both of them continue to enjoy sharing that story with others and laughing about it.

Humor helps us not to take ourselves and our problems too seriously. It helps us keep a perspective on things, allowing God to be God rather than trying to play God ourselves. A good laugh can help while we are waiting for the beginning. Ever notice how much better you feel after you have seen a funny movie or responded to laughter with your whole body from head to toe?

We do not have to be a bona fide comedian in order to laugh at ourselves. We all have a sense of humor that is God-given, and there are several good ways to maintain and develop it during times of stress and transition.

1. We can be alert to the incongruities and ironies of life. They are all about us and do not have to be blockbusters in order to leaven our life.

2. We can permit ourselves to smile. The little smile that starts in the corner of the mouth can spread, if we let it. Sometimes we feel as though we have to be serious in order to gain respect at work and to appear dignified. If that is what it takes to be respected and dignified, is it worth it?

3. We can read Norman Cousins's *Anatomy of an Illness* to see the value of humor in our lives, especially the healing qualities of humor. Cousins recounts his bout with a strange illness which did not respond to traditional medical treatment. He found that watching funny old movies and television shows provided relief from his pain.[7]

4. We can find other people who can laugh and have fun and deliberately choose to be with them when we need comic relief.

Talk to a Trained Person. When we run up against a block and cannot get on with our life, when we see that we have made a false start, or when the stress and anxiety get too high, we need the feedback of a wise and trusted friend, pastor, or counselor to provide us with some reality testing. In a major personal transition, if an internal beginning has not really begun to occur inside us within a period of one year after the external beginning took place, we need outside help.

A trained person can help us review other transitions of the past few years and the meaning of those events. As we share with such a person what we have been through and the ways in which we have coped, she or he may help us discover some areas we have overlooked which need to be opened up and dealt with. Those areas, or blind spots, may come from the ending and the wilderness we have recently experienced. They may, however, be related to our past. In either case, a trained person can help us sort out what is occurring.

Jack was contemplating making a major career change. Several friends suggested that he might want to take a deep look at all the roots of his need for such a change. He sought out a therapist and reviewed his life with her. In working out some unfinished business in relation to his recently deceased mother, Jack discovered even more powerfully than before that he needed to leave his present position in order to grow up. He saw in a new way how much his present job kept him in the position of being a momma's boy, something he had been aware of all his life. In order to separate from her and stand on his own two feet, he saw clearly that moving to a different kind of position was the necessary thing to do. The recent death of his mother had produced an internal ending which he was now able to identify.

An Internal Beginning Emerges

A real internal beginning is like experiencing the beginning of spring. One morning we notice a few birds singing in a way that they did not all winter long. A day occurs in which the sun announces that it has returned, and the skies are clear, and we think of spring. The very next day, snow and cold return, and the winds howl. After a few more cold wintry days, another springlike day comes. Then a crocus opens and we know for sure that spring is on the way.

An internal beginning occurs in fits and starts as well. The beginning is almost imperceptible in its silence, its gentleness, its initial signal. We may well miss the first chip on the egg from the baby chick inside, or the crocus shoot that first breaks ground. If we are open and alert, however, we will soon notice and then stand by in a kind of reverent awe at the new life that is occurring *in us!*—not to be announced to the world too quickly or to be rushed upon and trampled with our own attention. It is better to keep loving attention from a respectful distance as this fragile new thing emerges within.

We eventually respond with praise and thanksgiving, with celebration and joy. Since we know that we have not made it happen, we acknowledge that it is a gift of God. We do not own it, so we can only celebrate it as we accept it. Underneath all the cultural, social, familial, and church rituals around Christmas and Easter, perhaps the real significance of these two annual occasions is the reminder that hope and trust for a wonderful new possibility from God is available to each of us.

Our Bodies. In the phase of beginning, our bodies may feel rejuvenated, fresh, like an infant's body. While there is stress in adjusting to the new situation, we have had experience in coping with stress during the earlier phases. Especially if we are older, our bodies may respond during a new beginning in ways that we recall from earlier years. In effect, our bodies rise to the challenge of the new thing. Our bodies provide us with energy for the new.

Our Emotions. There may be some fear, but if we have worked through our blocks, we will usually feel excitement. The exhilaration of the new will help us deal with any initial hesitation. As we proceed further, the impact of the new beginning may sink in, so that we wonder what we have gotten ourselves into. As the implications of the beginning are lived into each day, however, our emotions will settle. We will then find ourselves in a better place emotionally, if we have gone through the phases well. We will feel more together, more whole, a deeper person for what happened—even if we did not ask for the transition.

Our Spirit. Our spiritual self will be in tune with God in a way that will generate spontaneous appreciation and thankfulness to God. We have followed God's leading through an ending, the chaotic middle phase, and into a beginning. While the beginning is no Garden of Eden, it is the right place for us at this time. If we have followed God and worked through the previous phases, we will feel that we are being transformed more into the likeness of God.

True beginnings happen in all kinds of ways. The following is a description of a dramatic, transforming beginning for Jane, whom we talked about earlier:

> *[After the spiritual retreat, I discovered that] I had opted for some things that were either new in my life or I had not had for a long time, or I had resisted, and five words/phrases sum this up: settled; stability; long-term; commitment; ground-of-being purpose for my life. Life is all of a sudden stable—which it hasn't been since before my father died. I discovered something fascinating about this stability: Once you are in it, you can see interesting possibilities, horizons, options you couldn't see till you were in it! . . .*
>
> *The astonishment that my life-work has presented itself before my eyes!—completely different from, more solid than, any previous life-work because it's made ground-of-being right by being grounded in the Ground-of-Being. . . . Awareness of a connection with God I haven't felt before (visual image: walking along an earth path in Psalm 23's "green pastures"). Have never before felt to this extent the strength of the rootedness, the rightness, of doing things for God: walking in that path now, not with a sense of emotion or feeling, but just of being in deep-down-below-feeling-level alignment.*
>
> *And lastly, the beautiful revelation before sleep: I was*

suddenly overcome by the most beautiful, serene, deep, graced peace—deeper than any peace I have ever known.

For Personal Reflection

Continue with the same transition that you worked with for the previous two chapters.

Did you experience a new beginning with that transition?
If you did not, what phase are you in at this time?
Is there a block?
What do you need to do in order to finish that transition?
If you did experience a new beginning, how did it occur?
Was there a feeling of thankfulness connected with it?
Was there an overlap with the ending, the wilderness, and the beginning?
Is there any unfinished business for you in this transition?
If you have regrets over earlier transitions that you would now do differently if you could, can you be gentle with yourself and forgive yourself? Can you say that you did the best you could, given the circumstances and the resources?
"Resolve to be always beginning—to be a beginner!"[8]

6

Growing Through Transitions: Resources for the Journey

All of life is caught up in motion and change. And because God is still creating, nothing that lives is finished or complete. To believe in a Living God is to recognize change as an inevitable dimension of life. Adapting to change is therefore a creative act as well as a necessity for survival.

—Herbert Anderson[1]

This final chapter will look at practical ways in which we can live through transitions so that growth occurs. While the chapters on each phase of a transition have included a section called Helps Along the Way, this chapter will take more of an overview concerning the resources available for our use throughout the entire process.

Recognizing the Internal Signals

Before we can use resources, we have to recognize that we are in a state of transition. If we pay attention to ourselves and our reactions, we can pick up the signals that a transition is occurring. Our bodies, minds, souls, and emotions respond in a variety of ways to the stress triggered by change. Following are common responses to the stress of intense personal change. If we are alert, each response prompts us to ask if this signals a transition occurring.

Panic. While panic is hard to ignore, it may be our first emotional response when the full import of a transition hits us, especially when a crisis occurs. To panic at some point in the process is not unusual and is commonly followed by a more calm period when we can strategize. It is important to remember that a panic attack does not last long, and from our experience we know that we can ride it out. Beyond the immediate feelings, we may be receiving a signal through the panic response that the front end of a transition has hit us.

To try to stifle the panic and pretend that we have things under control may mean we will fall apart later. Sometimes we need to maintain our poise in order to get through a crisis and then let go when it is safe, as Marjorie found when she was held up at gunpoint while working at a bank. She was calm and businesslike during the robbery; it was only after the robber left that she began to tremble and cry.

One result of panic is to freeze up. We stop dead in our tracks. We feel immobilized. Freezing is the way our bodies react when the trauma of change is too much to handle. As our thumb goes numb when it is first struck by a hammer, so our bodies and emotions may go numb when struck by unexpected news or events. Like the reaction of panic, freezing up usually passes. After President Kennedy was shot, people remember walking around in a dazed state; it was hard to believe at first.

Depression. At the beginning of a transition we may become depressed. Depression is one stage of the grief process and is to be expected whenever we deal with loss. Depression pushes us inside ourselves. Taken seriously rather than ignored, depression can ultimately be our friend. If we pay attention to the depression, it can tell us that something is wrong and help us deal with unfinished business. Depression, like pain, can motivate us to look at ourselves and search for the healing we need.

Depression, on the other hand, can be held on to and grow into a way of life. We know people who have been sad all their lives, the result of holding on to depression.

Anger. Anger is a common reaction during times of transition and may be the first indicator that a transition is beginning to occur. It can come from feeling helpless and out of control, or from having to deal with things with which we do not want to deal. Anger contains energy that can be mobilized to meet the challenge of the transition. Older adults, for example, who are in nursing homes live longer when they are feisty and refuse to conform to all the rules. On the other hand, we can wrap ourselves in our anger and refuse to move or grow.

Anxiety. Anxiety is a constant companion, so much so that we may not even be aware of it. During times of change, anxiety can heighten and intrude into our awareness and affect our bodies. It can press us to work on getting through the transition so that we return to a more relaxed state. Too much anxiety is unmanageable and becomes unproductive, while too little may not give us the edge we need to be creative. The person who effectively delivers a sermon on Sunday morning knows that the right amount of anxiety is a motivation.

Depression, anger, and anxiety are coping mechanisms of our body and need to be respected as signals of possible transitions. By paying attention to them, we may get clues for what we need to do. They can be used to point the way and to provide the energy for the work. Too much of any of the three feelings, however, can immobilize us. If that happens, we should find a trained helper to assist us with the feelings. In severe cases, we may need to see a psychiatrist or a medical doctor for medication, to help us get through a particularly rough time.

Managing the Stress

All the signals listed above are indicators that stress is present and affecting us. If we are in a deeply personal transition, the pressure will continue throughout the three phases and will hit peaks and valleys. While specific suggestions have been mentioned for dealing with stress during each phase, following are avenues we can consider in managing the strain.

Physical Dimensions. A healthful, balanced diet with little salt, sugar, and chemical preservatives is especially important during a time when we are under pressure. We need to be alert and energetic for meeting the complexities of transition. In order to do that, we need to provide the best possible nutrition for our bodies.

Exercising. Regular exercise is one of the best disciplines to maintain during a time of transition. The effects of exercise on the body, the mind, the emotions, and the spirit are beneficial. Studies of depression, for example, have shown that the body chemicals released during running provide a sense of well-being and euphoria. Exercise can also be combined with prayer or meditation, which can relieve the monotony of exercise while at the same time feeding our spiritual life.

Before we enter into a major transition or crisis, we should already have a routine of exercise in which we regularly engage. When difficult times come, we then do not have to go through the added stress of finding what exercise program best suits us.

Relaxing. Given the stress and intensity of a personal transition, we need to find times and ways to relax during the day, in addition to getting adequate sleep each night. Specific techniques of relaxation may be helpful, such as using a relaxation tape that provides a peaceful healing image, listening to music, walking slowly before bedtime, enjoying a sunset, birdwatching, watching television, or reading the newspaper. Whatever works is the strategy to use.

Intellectual Dimensions. Our intellect is a gift from God and is an important resource, both for understanding the specific nature of the change through which we are going and for considering the various options. The stress of change is easier to handle if we know what is going on and what alternatives we have. Education is an important resource in adapting to and implementing desired life changes. In addition, education gives a person more options by providing a broader range of employment opportunities.

Talking to a trained person is another way of providing options for our intellect to consider. While anxiety tends to put blinders on us, so that we see only a narrow area of reality in front of us, talking to a trusted pastor, friend, or counselor can broaden our field of vision.

Through sheer force of intellect some people are able to deal with extremely difficult situations. The intellect, in these cases, makes a primary contribution to survival.

Karl grew up in a home where his mother was repeatedly hospitalized for depression. His father was away a lot, working during the day and apparently spending time with another woman in the evening. With his superior intellect, Karl taught himself how to read before he began school and withdrew into the world of books. Now as an adult he does not possess well-developed social skills, but he did survive what could have been a devastating situation.

Be Curious. Our intellect can provide an attitude of patient curiosity that helps us learn from change and not run from it. We may say to ourselves, for example, "I've noticed myself being more irritable lately." From this observation, we can say, "Stop it! You're a nice person who should not do that." Or we can say, "Now I wonder what is going on that has me feeling this way." The second question gets our curiosity involved, so that we become a student of our responses rather than a judge of our actions.

This attitude of curiosity lives with the change in an observant way that is not passive. It can help us to live through the transition from a centered position inside ourselves or, more aptly stated, from having God in the center.

Reframe It. Reframing has to do with changing the way we look at a particular situation. Changing the way we view a problem will change our reaction. For example, to look at a crisis as an unprecedented learning opportunity rather than a terrible tragedy will make us less anxious and more open to looking at options.

You may have seen the puzzle that asks the reader to connect the dots contained within a rectangle by using only a certain number of lines. The problem can be solved only by extending the lines beyond the edges of the rectangle! Once we see that the edges of the old frame of a particular problem do not have to keep us boxed in, we are free to explore a wide variety of options.

In order to get outside the rectangle we have to distance ourselves from the chaos and intentionally let our minds play with possibilities. We have all had the experience of trying so hard to solve a problem that we missed the obvious answer. Detaching ourselves and pulling back can free our minds. The freedom inspires creativity, which allows us to listen to God and to our own deeper wells of inspiration.

Reframing can also help to affirm who we are and what we did in the situation, rather than looking only at the negative side. A young woman who gets her first job and moves out on her own may find that she does not make enough money to cover all her expenses. While moving back with her parents may feel like defeat, she can be helped to see that she *did* get a job, she did learn a great deal about budgeting and finances by being on her own, and she can make the next move from her parents a more permanent one.

Focus on What Is Possible. We may need to ignore certain difficulties in order to concentrate on others. We cannot work on everything at once. We may have to ignore the fact that we are overweight, our yard needs trimming, and our car is dirty while we are dealing with the death of a close friend.

A time of transition can have a ripple effect so that we reevaluate a number of areas of daily living. Changing a part that is simple to do may give us support to continue coping with the harder transition. Cleaning our closet, for example, takes less time and is easier to do than grieving for the death of a good friend. Cleaning the closet can make us feel good, especially if it is something we've thought of doing for a long time. Making more space in our closet may symbolize an attempt to make inner space for other friends and activities.

Emotional Dimensions. The stress of transitions affects our emotions. The way we deal with these feelings can help us manage stress. Following are some constructive possibilities.

Vent Feelings. Deep feelings are stirred at each stage of change. They are important to recognize and to express, either privately or to a trustworthy person in a safe setting. Yelling and crying are two ways that strong feelings can be vented. Yelling in a place where others will not hear can be a great release of pent-up emotions. As a result, our bodies will not have to express the feelings for us in ways that can make us sick, and we are more clearheaded in working through the transition.

Parents, for example, may receive the news with ambivalence that their adult child is engaged to be married. For a variety of reasons, there may be negative feelings about this major change. The raw, uncensored feelings need to be expressed to the other parent or to a trusted friend. Verbally expressing the negative feelings in tactful yet clear ways to the son or daughter can then help both parents find positive feelings about the event.

Laugh at It. Laughter can be an important strategy that provides welcome relief and a momentary disengagement that may offer a new perspective. Taking ourselves too seriously narrows our view and stifles our creativity. The stress of personal change often means that we make more mistakes and are less coordinated. Feeling bad about the mistakes only adds to the stress, while laughing at them releases pent-up energy and helps us to get on with living.

Indulge Yourself. Caring for ourselves with small indulgences during a difficult time of transition can be a way of taking care of ourselves and surviving. For example, one person enjoys soaking in a hot bath when she is under stress. This brings back pleasant memories from her childhood. On the other hand, indulging ourselves can be another way to ignore the problems.

Appreciate Yourself. It is important to make a conscious effort to hold in our awareness any successes, no matter how small, in dealing with the transition. Recalling other transitions successfully handled can also help. Appreciating ourselves can be a powerful shaper of our perspective on the world and the meaning we give to any situation. Feeling inadequate can make a problem appear impossible to solve, while appreciating ourselves can give us the energy to explore options and move ahead.

Reward Yourself. Rewarding ourselves can be an important way of managing stress. Finding little rewards along the way, plus a large one at the end, can help provide a different perspective on the transition we are undergoing. The path will not look so dark and dreary.

These last four suggestions are ways of being gentle with ourselves. Being hard on ourselves only adds to the stress we are already experiencing from a transition.

Social Dimensions. Our social network provides an important resource for support during times of transition. Friends, faith community, extended family, nuclear family, spouse, relationships at work—all are potential resources during times of stress and transition.

Sometimes we have difficulty in receiving help and knowing how much to allow others to support us. If we are dependent, we may want others to take too much care of us. If others attempt to solve the problem for us, we are weakened to that extent and made more dependent.

Independent types are uncomfortable with the vulnerability of receiving and will probably not allow others to support them. Knowing ourselves and our particular style can reveal which tendency we have. Listening to feedback from our friends and from our own best judgment will tell us if we are leaning too much or not enough. One study of 50 clerical workers found that 50 percent of those involved in a transition with a spouse believed that they had relied too little on others. On the other hand, 25 percent, involved in geographic moves, believed that they relied on others too much.[2]

Help from others in the form of information, feedback, support, exploring options, and prayer can be useful during a transition.

> Rowena recalls with gratitude the time she asked her church for help with her children. Her mother had cancer and was in the hospital in a neighboring city. During the final months of the illness, the church provided child care so that Rowena could make regular trips to be with her mother.

Withdraw. Even extroverts may find that they need time to be by themselves. Withdrawing from some normal activities, cutting back on some commitments, spending time alone—all can be helpful when we are going through certain stages of a transition. However, the constant use of withdrawal will ultimately not solve anything and probably will make the situation more difficult.

Talk. Alternating with withdrawal are times that we need to talk. Talking can provide important feedback, support, a check on our perceptions, an unloading of feelings—among other things. Talking constantly, however, not only wears out our friends but also can be used to avoid action.

Spiritual Dimensions. While some people think of God only as a last resort, turning to God can be as natural as turning to others for help. On the down side, it can be a cop-out from facing our own responsibility, or it can be a search for a magical solution. Not using this resource, however, means that we lose the insight, support, and grounding that is available from God. God's love can surround us, God's challenge can help keep us honest, and God's call can lure us into the unknown future.

We are not creatures who simply draw from experiences in the past. Our hopes, visions, and commitments affect our dealing with personal transitions in the present and emerge from our spiritual center.

Hope. Our faith in God provides hope, which gives meaning and direction to living in the present as well as to facing the future. Out of our spiritual depths come hopes and dreams for ourselves, our children, and perhaps for the world.

If parents hope to provide a better life for their children than they themselves had, then moving to a new location for the sake of a higher-paying job will make the transition easier for the parents. The children, who may not share in that goal, may have trouble with the move, especially if it comes at the time of a developmental transition for them.

Vision. To religious persons, a deeply held vision of the way things can be is a gift from God. This vision provides a gyroscope that keeps us on course through changes and difficult times. Persons who have the vision of a more just and peaceful world seem to be able to endure profound hardships in pursuit of that vision. It provides them with a power to move through transitions without allowing the changes to defeat them. This does not mean, of course, that persons in activist causes never get tired and never need to pay attention to their personal needs. It does testify to the great power and focus with which a dream about the future can provide us. A great deal of chaos resulting from transition can be handled if there is *meaning* to what is happening. Our vision can provide the meaning that is a grounding point in dealing with transitions.

Burnout is not so much a result of overwork as a result of a loss of vision and the hope that makes it possible. "Where there is no vision, the people perish" (Prov. 29:18a, KJV). The cure for this burnout is worship. In authentic worship, vision will be restored to us as we are called by God into the future.

Commitments. Likewise, our commitments come from our spiritual center and can be a resource during transitions. Our commitment to God can be the primary anchor in the midst of all the changes and turmoil of daily living. The psalms especially reflect this security, as shown in Psalm 121:7–8: "Yahweh guards you from all harm; Yahweh guards your life, Yahweh guards your comings and goings, henceforth and for ever."

Assuming that our commitments are authentic and connected with our deeper values, these commitments can serve as lifelines to hold on to during times of turmoil and stress. Our commitment to our marriage, for example, may help us through times of difficulty in the relationship with our spouse. If our commitment is not firm and clear, the result may be that it is easier to give up and leave the marriage than to stay and do the hard work.

Organizing Center. Our spiritual life has many effects on us and may be the organizing center around which coping resources are gathered. Life cultivated in God can provide grounding and concrete resources that are available to us during times of stress and transition. The religious practices that help during change depend on our personal history and may include such activities as silent meditation, prayer, reading scripture and religious books, listening to or singing spiritually moving music, keeping a journal, talking to a spiritual friend or guide, or joining in religious activities in our community of faith.

The worship of God provides a point of grounding outside ourselves that can place changes in perspective. In worship, we are in a posture of listening to God, so that God's call to us can be heard and then acted on. God can call us into some new place—if we perceive it. If God initiates the change, then faith enables us to trust that God will provide the gifts necessary for us to follow God's call and complete the change. Knowing that God has called us into this situation provides new energy and motivation for moving through it.

Strategies for Coping with Transitions

If we have recognized the transition and are managing the stress associated with it, we are then ready to deal directly with the change. Here are suggested strategies for coping with transitions.

Get Information and Advice. Our first strategy should be to obtain solid information on the specific kind of transition; the personal, interpersonal, and community resources; and the possible alternatives. The importance of correct information in dealing with change is so obvious it is easy to overlook. Our anxiety is compounded when we do not know what is going on. When something appears wrong with our bodies, for example, we need to get an accurate diagnosis of the problem. Once the diagnosis is made, the various options for treatment are then considered. Again, we need information as to the possible benefits, liabilities, cost, and availability of each option, in order to make an informed decision. Once the treatment is begun, information needs to flow regularly between us and the treatment team.

It is important to seek the advice of friends and persons who might have specialized knowledge that we need. Seeking advice involves deciding whom to ask, how to present our problem, and what to ask. Each of these decisions affects the kind of opinions and guidance we will receive. The opinion of others can never replace our own thoughtful consideration, but it can be a helpful supplement.

Review Alternatives. After obtaining the best possible information, reviewing the alternatives is an important step in forming a strategy for coping. As was seen in the last example, reviewing alternatives goes along with obtaining information.

Reflect. Reflection upon the information gained, the alternatives presented, and the inner resources available provides a calm center as we go through the whirlwind. A crucial coping mechanism for times of transition is the ability to consider inwardly where we are, what we are feeling, what we want from

life, what our values are, and a host of other insights that
self-reflection provides. Without self-reflection, we stumble
through change, learn nothing from it, and live life on the
surface. Experience, when reflected upon, is the basis for growth
and for wisdom.

Use Resources. As this chapter tries to make clear, we have
many resources, more than we are aware of, which reside within
ourselves, our relationships with others, and our relationship
with God. In addition, community and governmental agencies
and our community of faith have a wide variety of resources that
are available. As we use these resources, we will be working to
modify the transition.

Assert Yourself. Actively dealing with a transition may involve asserting ourselves. We never have to be totally passive
victims in dealing with any transition. Making decisions and
acting on them involve self-assertion. There is a time to act and
a time to wait, as we talked about earlier. We can assert ourselves too quickly or too slowly, either of which impedes the
transition process. Prayerfully discerning what is appropriate
for this time in our lives is basic for every phase of a transition.

Try to Change the Situation. Working to change the situation can mean rearranging extraneous parts so that we can focus
on the major problem. We also may work to make our situation
more livable during a transition. While we are working, for
example, on a more equal and satisfying marriage relationship,
we may want to change our living situation by cutting back on
civic commitments, not assuming new responsibilities at work,
and making more time to be together with our spouse.

Mori and Amy came for marriage counseling because Amy
was unhappy with their lack of intimacy. Mori was willing to
come along because he was committed to the marriage and
felt he loved Amy. As they began to work on their relationship and explore the roots of their communication patterns in
their own childhood families, they found that, though the

process consumed a great deal of time and energy, it was important enough to both of them that they gave priority to it. They had to use some of their savings in order to pay for the counseling. In addition, Amy decided not to accept a promotion at work which would have meant being away from home several days each month. Likewise, Mori turned down the offer to be president of the civic association. After a year of concentrated work, their marriage and their personal lives were more fulfilling.

Confront It. Facing into the transition is the strategy that is often advocated in this book. It has the advantage of using the least amount of energy in the least amount of time, in order to get through the period of transition. It is efficient.

Geri felt a lump in her breast that was uncomfortable when touched. When it did not go away in a couple of weeks, she made an appointment with her medical doctor, who checked her, sent her for a mammogram, and concluded that the lump was not malignant but that it should be watched. The doctor suggested that Geri perform a monthly self-examination and return in six months for another medical examination and mammogram, explaining that breast cancer found in its early stages is easier to cure. Even though no cancer was found, Geri was glad she had not postponed seeing her doctor.

Responses to Avoid

In order to grow as a result of a transition, the following responses should usually be avoided, especially when used to the extreme. Sometimes, however, there may be a limited usefulness for a specific response. Again, our inner discernment and the feedback of others are needed.

Denial. All of us use denial as a way of coping, especially if there appears to be nothing we can do to change the situation. Without denial, the constant awareness of our mortality could immobilize us. A student met with me recently and was expressing anxiety about his summer plans, but he ended with the statement, "But I'm really doing all right." I replied, "Sounds like good denial to me," and we both laughed.

Continuing to use denial, however, when there are positive actions we can take means that we are limiting our ability to cope. We may need the honest feedback of friends to break through this kind of denial.

Running Away. This is a specific kind of denial in which we focus our attention on something else. "Out of sight, out of mind" is the guiding maxim for this strategy. Like denial, running away may be just what we need to do for a while—in order to catch our breath, rest, and collect our thoughts. For example, it is important for parents to "run away" for dinner and a movie, or some kind of brief vacation, while they are dealing with a child who is having problems.

To continue to run away can cause the original problem to become ingrained and larger, which makes it even more difficult to handle. In turn, the growing problem may increase our reluctance to break through the denial and tackle it. The vicious circle gains momentum.

Resigning Too Soon. We may feel like a victim of circumstances, or of others' actions toward us, and take a passive stance. "It must be God's will, so I have to accept it" is the religious expression of this position. Given our limited years and resources, resignation is appropriate in some situations, but *not* until we have tried all other avenues of approach. If resignation occurs too early in the process, again we are copping out.

Suicide. This is the most desperate response to crisis, but one which some feel called upon to use. Are there times when suicide might be appropriate in a given circumstance? While this question is debated today, many persons of Christian faith believe that God gives life and only God has the right to take it away. To commit suicide is to play God. This may be one strategy that is never appropriate, although the thought may occur to us. The thought of suicide is a sign that a person needs help in dealing with desperation.

Staying Busy. Becoming involved in activities can be a helpful break in dealing with an intense period in our lives. If used constantly, of course, the busyness becomes a way of not dealing with personal issues. Turning to areas where we feel competent and confident is alluring during a transition when we are feeling insecure. There are always areas that ask for our attention. We can find many ways to feel good about not dealing with a transition.

Harboring Detrimental Attitudes. The following are common attitudes that cause us more harm than good in our attempts to pay attention to, work through, and learn from our transitions. We learn them in a variety of subtle and not-so-subtle ways, in society and in faith communities.

"The sooner I get on with things, after a crisis or change, the better it is." Our society tends to encourage us to move on as quickly as possible, and our faith communities may also subscribe to this value. At the time of death of a family member, we are cared for during the time of the funeral and for a few days afterward. A month or so later, we begin to receive messages, such as "It's time to put it behind you," that encourage us to get out and stop dwelling on the loss. Until recently, we as a country have prided ourselves on being a young country that does not look back. The "fast forward" button found on videocassette recorders and tape recorders exemplifies the way we live our lives.

As we have seen, this attitude makes us reluctant to pay attention to our inner processes during a transition. We may attempt to ignore what is going on inside us or we may get on with the next stage so quickly that we jump over the griefwork and middle phase. The price we pay is either a superficial style of life, which prevents us from relating deeply over a period of time, or a series of failed relationships and unhappy chapters in our lives. Ecclesiastes reminds us that there is a time to mourn and a time to dance (3:4).

"If we indulge ourselves, we will want more and more and never get on with life." The underlying view of human nature here is that we are basically lazy and dependent creatures who, if given a chance, will let others take care of us. This attitude,

though not spoken directly, is often held by strong, independent people who have had to take care of themselves and thus may have had to repress their own neediness.

If we are close to someone going through a transition, we may get tense if the person begins to lean on us too much during a time of transition. It is understandable that we may not have the time or emotional energy that a person in crisis needs. We can deal with our own limits by getting others in the community involved.

On the other hand, there is a kind of condescending care that keeps the receiver dependent. In these cases, our need to be needed, and important, is the problem. In contrast, good care is like tasty, emotional spinach; it makes us strong and robust.

"I have to do it on my own. Others may listen, but in the final analysis it is my life." While it is true that our life is our own and we make our own decisions, it is equally true that our life occurs within community, and our decisions are made in the context of the time, place, and people in which we live. We look at only one half of the equation when we look at our solitariness. Men in our culture, with the additional message that they have to be strong and independent, are especially crippled by such a viewpoint.

This attitude prevents us from using the resources and help that are available. We end up depriving ourselves of support and direction. We go hungry in a room full of food.

Giving and receiving are two basic modes of human interaction; each carries difficulties which can be experienced during the stress of transition, as shown in these last two attitudes. Asking for help or receiving help can be seen as weakness. We do not like to be seen as weak and needy, so we may put on a mask of strength when we are in a crisis of transition.

"Human worth is determined by income, title, kind of house, address, car, clothes, professional status—or something that we do or buy." This attitude is so much a part of our daily living that it is difficult to be aware of it. If we have trouble relaxing on weekends, over holidays, or during our vacation, we would do well to ask ourselves if we are being driven to validate our worth through what we do. If we feel good only by helping others, we may wonder if we gain worth solely by doing.

Our faith community, while saying that God loves everyone, may act as though God loves the successful a little more. The car we drive, the clothes we wear, the house we live in may reflect God's blessings on us. (Of course it is easy then to say that the poor deserve to be that way.)

This attitude makes it difficult, if not impossible, to look seriously at our personhood. We focus so on what we accomplish that we are unable to look at who we are and what is going on inside us. We become anxious when we sense that our time is up in a job; we cannot allow ourselves the leisure of a middle phase, when we may be out of work for a while or may not know what direction to pursue. Since a wrong direction is easier to live with than the anxiety of no direction, we dash off in any direction on the compass.

Evelyn Underhill, who writes with wisdom concerning the spiritual life, states the point well:

> We mostly spend [our] lives conjugating three verbs: to Want, to Have, and to Do. Craving, clutching, and fussing . . . we are kept in perpetual unrest. . . . Being, not wanting, having, and doing, is the essence of a spiritual life.[3]

Messages to Remember

The messages we tell ourselves make a great difference in our ability to deal with a situation. Telling ourselves that the situation is unimportant or not as life-threatening as we fear, for example, can help us to see the difficulty with different eyes. While self-talk can alleviate stress, it can also change our perception of the transition by reminding ourselves of the reality of *this* situation. If we are overreacting to the present transition, we must be bringing feelings from another area into this one. Self-talk can help us stay focused on the present by reminding us of the way this situation is different from others. The following messages are especially important to tell ourselves during stressful times.

We are accepted. The crucial question that presses on us when we find ourselves in transition is whether our community will continue to accept us, both while we are in the process of change and after we have changed. We feel different inside and may well relate differently to others. Are others going to like us and accept the way we now are? Do we still belong? Will they hang in there with us during this time?

Communities and friends will give us a variety of messages in this area. A healthy community of faith will fairly consistently convey to us that we are acceptable. If your community does not accept you, find one that does. The crucial point to remember, however, is that we are accepted by God and are therefore enabled to accept ourselves.

"We are the temple of the living God" (2 Cor. 6:16b, RSV). This basic attitude makes listening to our bodies and attending to our inner processes a spiritual act. Loving our bodies becomes one dimension of loving God. To go inside ourselves and inquire as to what is going on can be like returning to a beloved temple where we have met and worshiped God many times in our lives. It is like returning home.

Loving ourselves is not selfish, but a first step toward wholeness. In Matthew, Jesus says, "You must love your neighbour as yourself" (22:39; similarly in Lev. 19:18). Selfishness is not love; it comes from a lack of the right kind of love. Selfishness is a self-centeredness that is normal for infants and small children. With the right kind of nurture we grow beyond our small circle to include others and the world in our love. When it happens that way, enough self-centeredness remains to help us take care of ourselves and prevent us from allowing others to abuse us. Always thinking of others first is just as bad as always thinking of ourselves first. Healthy love aids us in maintaining the balance between attention to self and to others. Faith in God can provide the center to our lives that helps us keep this balance.

During times of upheaval and great transition, we may need to pay more attention to ourselves and to taking care of our inner processes. This does not mean that we will stay pulled back. We are going inward for the sake of going through the transition, so that we can emerge healed and ready to continue on the next leg of the journey. We can then be much more giving to others.

It is okay to ask for help. For those of us who were taught to be strong and self-sufficient, it is hard to ask. To ask implies need, and we are not supposed to need. We know that we are only creatures and therefore are limited, but we act as though we are God and need nothing.

It is okay to be strong. On the other side, some of us are afraid we will not be loved if we are strong and independent. We wonder if our faith community will ignore us and our friends feel we do not need them. The truth is, even though we are limited creatures, we have many gifts and we are adults. In spite of our wounds and blind sides, we have areas of wholeness and sight. Especially during a transition when we feel most weak, we need to remember our strength. Our strength will be attractive to other strong, healthy people.

We are passing on the love we have received from God. In many ways we experience that God "supports us in every hardship, so that we are able to come to the support of others, in every hardship of theirs because of the encouragement that we ourselves receive from God" (2 Cor. 1:4). The triangle of life is clear, in that the love and comfort flow from God to us and others, and we love God in return. Our aim in receiving love, then, is for our care and healing. When our healing has occurred, we can then pass it on.

> Janet was working in a local church as a student intern. She needed some remedial plastic surgery but couldn't afford it. When the church offered to pay for it, she was at first overwhelmed by their generosity and a bit reluctant to accept so large a gift. Janet was told that she should accept it now, in the knowledge that she could pass on the benefits of her increased self-esteem and appearance in her ministry, and might someday be able to provide similar medical help to another person. Reframing the meaning of accepting the offer enabled her to accept the generous gift.

The world is torn and hurting. When we are healed to some extent and are not in a major transition, we are sensitive to the wounds of others, as well as to the problems of the world, and become involved in helping.

We are both like and different from everyone else. My similarity to everyone else makes me feel part of a common humanity. We are truly in this together. During a transition, however, we need especially to remember that we are different in what we need. Therefore, the kind of care has to be shaped to fit our need at this point in our lives.

Sometimes, such as when we have experienced a recent death in our family, we need the community to gather and show its care and support. We need the assurance that we still are part of the community even though we have suffered a major loss. Other times in the same grief process we will need to have private time. Caring means neither hovering nor disregarding, but a middle way that avoids both extremes. Caring involves basic respect for us.

Each stage of a transition requires different kinds of caring. The caring needed cannot be prescribed beforehand. Rather, we who are going through the transition will have to say what we need at any given time. The task of others is to be available and guided in their caring by our expressed wishes. The community cannot read minds; therefore, it is our responsibility to tell what is needed at each point, insofar as we know. If the community members jump in with what they *think* is caring, the action may come across as intrusive or controlling.

On the other hand, we do not always know what we need at a particular moment. In that case, one hopes the community can exercise patience, be present in a nondemanding way, hold us in prayer, and be sensitive in attempting to elicit indications of what we need. Simple acts—like writing a note or bringing a flower or offering to keep the children one afternoon—convey love to us in a nonintrusive, noncontrolling way.

Support from Our Faith Community

Our faith communities, if we attend a church, synagogue, or meeting, can provide important resources, guidance, and support during times of transition. Listed here are a few of the important ways that communities of faith can be an influence for good.

Education. Education can help us both before a major transition occurs and during such a time. Education is one of the most important ways that faith communities can prepare us for transitions. A faith community can make us aware that each of us goes through a variety of transitions; that transitions are normal and, as such, are not to be feared; that transitions, rather than being rushed through, need a kind of spiritual attention that makes it possible for us to hear the voice of God at different points; that we will feel loss and grief, and that griefwork has its own cycle; that anxiety is present and to be expected; that watching and waiting are necessary.

We can obtain this education in a variety of ways: for example, in the structured educational program of the faith community. If we need specific information, we can find instruction in the Christian education program, such as a Sunday morning study group; through workshops and retreats on a variety of topics; and in sermons, books, and conferences.

The most important education, however, may occur informally through the attitudes and behaviors of the members of the community. The life of the community will be informed by their attitudes as the faith community stays alert for the real-life needs of all of us who attend. We learn as we live together.

Rites of Passage. Rites of passage are ritualized ways that communities help us move through the different phases of transitions. Through rites of passage a community can acknowledge and participate in our transitions. When going through transitions, we feel supported by the rituals and receive assurance that we remain members in good standing of the community. Thus rituals act as bridges that help us traverse chasms in the land of change.

We usually find rites of passage in faith communities for marriage, the birth of children, entrance into the faith community, and death. In faith communities that practice believers' baptism, the ritual of baptism and subsequent partaking of the Lord's Supper are markers of our entrance into the age of accountability. If we are sick, listing our name in the church bulletin is a ritualized way of including us in the life of the community and asking for prayers and expressions of concern.

In many communities a rosebud near the altar celebrates the birth of a baby. Faith communities generally have a ritualized way of welcoming us, if we are visitors, to their services of worship. Also included may be a welcome if we are returning after a period of illness or hospitalization.

We are not likely to find public rites of passage in faith communities for transitions of divorce, entrance into the teen years, graduation from high school, leaving for college or the military, mid-life, changing jobs, entering older adulthood, or leaving the faith community. Faith communities do not generally have rituals for the negative events in our lives. This lack creates the impression that we have to be happy and nice in order to belong to a community of faith. If this is the case, we certainly do not feel comfortable in bringing our problems to the community.

Divorce is one of the most painful events in people's lives. Yet those of us who divorce often feel a lack of support from our faith community, even though we may have been active church leaders. In some cases we feel judgment and end up leaving the community out of guilt, anger, or frustration. On the other hand, some faith communities are beginning to offer "unwedding" ceremonies to persons who are getting a legal divorce. A public ritual of some kind could signify to us that God and the faith community have not abandoned us, as well as teaching others in the faith community to be more accepting. Loving and accepting those who are divorcing does not necessarily mean that blanket approval is being given to the act of divorce.

We may feel the need of rituals to help us mark our personal transitions. Our faith community can be helpful. However, if we fall into one of the foregoing categories that faith communities tend to ignore, we may want to talk with our minister about an appropriate ritual. We can also devise our own ritual and invite our close friends to join in its observance.

> Georgia had been through a difficult time of marital problems and then separation. When her divorce became final, she decided to invite her closest friends to go out to dinner. The time together gave them a chance to talk about the past, ritually mark the change in status for Georgia, and celebrate

the beginning of a new stage in her life. Later, she reflected that the dinner had been more significant than she could have anticipated.

Groups. We find that a great deal of caring in faith communities occurs before and after meetings, on the telephone, and through cards and letters if we are hospitalized or suffering a major loss. In addition, there are a number of ongoing groups in any faith community where attention and care are given to us and to others in transition. Christian education classes are a natural place for both education and support to take place. If the classes are age-graded, each class will probably have persons going through similar transitions, although individual differences and contexts provide a unique flavor.

Social times within faith communities provide opportunities for acknowledgment of our major transitions. Women's and men's groups that are formed for a variety of purposes, along with prayer and support groups, are places where we can find care and support as we undergo changes in our lives.

In addition, special groups can be formed for the specific purpose of supporting us and others in transition. In one church to which I belonged, a group for parents of adolescents was started out of the minister's need for support in dealing with difficulties with his oldest son. A support group for parents of elementary school children has more recently been started, as well as a group for persons in transition. Those who are in the process of becoming single again seem to be using this group the most.

If we find such a transition group, it makes a statement to us that transitions are okay, that we are accepted in the community during our times of change and crisis, and that a resource is available for us to use, if we desire. As a result, we feel included in the community of faith.

If we are in a significant transition and our faith community does not have a support group of some kind for us, perhaps another faith community in the area does. If not, we could help to start one, if we have the energy and the "inner leading" to do so.

Guides. In addition to providing education, support groups, and rituals, the loving faith community can offer mentors or guides for us and others who are traversing the rocky shoals of change. We need a steady person with whom to stay in contact. While the trained, sensitive pastor may be that person, others in the faith community may show particular gifts and abilities in standing by us during change. Persons who themselves have worked through major transitions, and are in a stable place, may have a special sensitivity and understanding to offer those of us who are in the middle of a transition now. They then join the long line of "wounded healers," persons who minister out of their woundedness.

An important task for the pastor is to become aware of such persons in the faith community, affirm their God-given gifts and experience, and help them use these gifts for the upbuilding of the community. As the pastor becomes aware of persons in transition, she or he can introduce those persons to others in the congregation who can be of help. Besides relieving the pastor of some responsibility, this ministry of introduction can help to actualize the ministry of all Christians.[4]

Some members of the faith community may be especially sensitive in the spiritual area. They could be encouraged to obtain training for being spiritual guides for others. The Shalem Institute in Washington (Mount St. Alban, Washington, DC 20016) and Wainwright House in Rye, New York (260 Stuyvesant Avenue, Rye, NY 10580) are two places where training is available. You yourself may want to consider pursuing such training after you have completed your transition. "In our movement into the mystery of God everything that has happened to us is potential gift: our wounds, our disappointments, our idiosyncrasies, and our failures."[5]

If you are in a period of deep transition and your faith community is important to you, talk with your minister about someone who could serve as a guide during this time. Trained spiritual guides are becoming more numerous in this country. Calling one of the two places just listed could tell you if a graduate of its program lives in your area. A religious retreat center near you could also give you names of such persons.

For Personal Reflection

Using your lifeline graph from chapter 2, consider the following questions:

What were the signals that your major transitions were beginning?

How did you manage the stress?

What strategies did you use to cope with the major transitions?

How well did they work, in retrospect?

Are there other strategies described in this chapter, or identified through your reflection, you wish you had tried?

What do you need to avoid and what messages do you need to remember the next time you experience a deep transition? You may want to keep the answer to this question in a place where you can refer to it later.

In what ways was your community of faith supportive of you during your transitions? In what ways was it not supportive?

Now take a step back and reflect on your life. What strikes you as you look at your chart? You may see for the first time how much your life has been like a roller coaster, or you may be impressed with how smooth your life has been so far. Some people, in reflecting on their lifelines, are struck by how many of their transitions have both positive and negative memories attached to them.

After you complete this exercise, you may want to share your lifeline with a person you are close to. If other people complete a similar project, the mutual sharing can heighten the meaningfulness and provide learning for everyone.

Epilogue

Endings and beginnings are hard, and the in-between phase can be even harder. At the same time that they are hard, they are also wonderfully exhilarating and can renew and transform us. As this book draws to a close, you will be going on with your life and I will be ending a writing project that has consumed a major portion of time and energy. I will be ready for new beginnings after a wilderness time of rest and reflection, and you too will be ready for new beginnings. We both will be living lives where endings will continue to occur, whether or not we are aware of them or like them. We will find ourselves in chaos and after a while discover firm ground beneath our feet. But if we—

> Listen to the voice of God speaking to us
> Attend to our bodies, minds, emotions, and spirits
> Draw on the resources of our families, friends, and communities of faith
> Have patience, curiosity, and a sense of humor—

we will make it through: enlivened, enriched, thankful, perhaps wiping the sweat off our brow.

Then we will be ready, when the day comes, for our final transition: when we die. It too, I am convinced, has the same three phases. We know something about the ending of life, because we have grieved over the loss of others through death. We will know about the ending in a different way when we ourselves die. Then will come a middle time, after which we in some way will find ourselves on the firm ground of the loving presence of God, in a glorious new beginning. The final transition will have happened. We will be transformed into the likeness of God.

Notes

Chapter 1: Invitation to the Journey

1. Elizabeth O'Connor, *Cry Pain, Cry Hope,* pp. 13–14. (Where the full facts of publication are omitted, they may be found in the reading list.)

2. Alan Jones, *Exploring Spiritual Direction* (New York: Seabury Press, 1982), p. 18.

Chapter 2: The Dimensions of Transitions

1. Lewis Carroll, *Alice's Adventures in Wonderland* (New York: Oxford University Press, 1971), pp. 40–41.

2. Ivan Charner and Nancy K. Schlossberg, "Variations by Theme: The Life Transitions of Clerical Workers," *Vocational Guidance Quarterly* 34:4 (June 1986), p. 213.

3. Harold Kushner, *Why Bad Things Happen to Good People* (New York: Schocken Books, 1981).

4. Viktor Frankl, *The Doctor and the Soul* (New York: Alfred A. Knopf, 1965), pp. 105–106.

5. Judith Viorst, *Necessary Losses,* p. 285.

6. Edwin H. Friedman, *Generation to Generation: Family Process in Church and Synagogue* (New York: Guilford Press, 1985).

7. Erik Erikson, *Identity and the Life Cycle* (New York: International Universities Press, 1959), pp. 55–56.

8. Daniel Levinson, *Seasons of Man's Life* (New York: Ballantine Books, 1978), p. 53.

Chapter 3: The First Phase: Endings

1. Judith Viorst, *Necessary Losses,* p. 368.

2. Lewis Sherrill, *The Struggle of the Soul* (New York: Macmillan Co., 1963), p. 6.

3. James W. Fowler, *Becoming Adult, Becoming Christian: Adult Development and Christian Faith* (San Francisco: Harper & Row, 1984), p. 103.

4. Mark Pilgrim, "And a Time to Die," in Reuben Job and Norman Shawchuck, *A Guide to Prayer for Ministers and Other Servants* (Nashville: Upper Room, 1983), p. 56.

5. Kenneth R. Mitchell and Herbert Anderson, *All Our Losses, All Our Griefs* (Philadelphia: Westminster Press, 1983), p. 127.

6. C. S. Lewis, *A Grief Observed* (New York: Seabury Press, 1961), p. 46.

7. Ibid., p. 47.

8. See *Living with Oneself and Others* (New England Yearly Meeting, 1985), pp. 50–55, for further information about a structure and procedures that can be used in communities of faith.

9. Hugh Barbour, *The Quakers in Puritan England* (New Haven, Conn.: Yale University Press, 1964), pp. 119–122.

Chapter 4: The Second Phase: The Wilderness

1. Thomas Merton, *Contemplative Prayer* (Garden City, N.Y.: Doubleday & Co., Image Books, 1971), p. 24.

2. Robert L. Cohn, *The Shape of Sacred Space: Four Biblical Studies* (Chico, Calif.: Scholars Press, 1981), pp. 7–23.

3. Ibid., p. 14.

4. Kathleen Parker, "Anxiety May Cause Illness," *Cincinnati Enquirer,* October 18, 1987, p. H-9.

5. Cohn, *The Shape of Sacred Space,* p. 18.

6. William Bridges, *Transitions,* p. 119.

7. See, for example, Ignatius Loyola, *The Spiritual Exercises of Saint Ignatius,* tr. by Anthony Mottola (Garden City, N.Y.: Doubleday & Co., Image Books, 1958), and Teresa of Avila, *Interior Castle,* in *The Collected Works,* vol. 2, tr. by Kieran Kavanaugh and Otilio Rodriguez (Washington, D.C.: Institute of Carmelite Studies, 1980).

8. Augustine, *Confessions* (New York: Penguin Books, 1969).

9. Harry Emerson Fosdick, *The Living of These Days* (New York: Harper & Row, 1956), pp. 72–73.

10. Erik Erikson, *Identity and the Life Cycle* (New York: International Universities Press, 1959), p. 111.

11. Martha Courtot, in Linda Clark et al., *Image-Breaking, Image-Building: A Handbook for Creative Worship with Women of Christian Tradition* (New York: Pilgrim Press, 1981), pp. 75–76.

12. Alan Jones, *Soul Making,* p. 130.

13. For the ideas in these last two paragraphs, I am indebted to Bryan Harness.

14. John Sanford, *God's Forgotten Language* (Philadelphia: J. B. Lippincott Co., 1968), is a suggested book to read if you want to learn more about your dreams. ✳

Chapter 5: The Third Phase: Beginnings

1. Robert L. Cohn, *The Shape of Sacred Space: Four Biblical Studies* (Chico, Calif.: Scholars Press, 1981), p. 16.

2. Daniel Levinson, *Seasons of a Man's Life* (New York: Ballantine Books, 1978), p. 57.

3. Martha Courtot, in Linda Clark et al., *Image-Breaking, Image-Building: A Handbook for Creative Worship with Women of Christian Tradition* (New York: Pilgrim Press, 1981), p. 54.

4. Anne Wilson Schaef, *Co-Dependence: Misunderstood—Mistreated* (San Francisco: Harper & Row, Winston Press, 1986), p. 44.

5. Andrew Keegan, "Failure: The Ultimate Taboo," *Guideposts,* September 10, 1987, p. 6.

6. Emmet Fox, "Your Heart's Desire," in Reuben Job and Norman Shawchuck, *A Guide to Prayer for Ministers and Other Servants* (Nashville: Upper Room, 1983), p. 44.

7. Norman Cousins, *Anatomy of an Illness* (New York: W. W. Norton & Co., 1979).

8. John J. L. Mood, *Rilke on Love and Other Difficulties* (New York: W. W. Norton & Co., 1975), p. 25.

Chapter 6: Growing Through Transitions: Resources for the Journey

1. Herbert Anderson, *The Family and Pastoral Care* (Philadelphia: Fortress Press, 1984), p. 31.

2. Ivan Charner and Nancy K. Schlossberg, "Variations by Theme: The Life Transitions of Clerical Workers," *Vocational Guidance Quarterly* 34:4 (June 1986), p. 221.

3. Evelyn Underhill, "The Spiritual Life," in Reuben Job and Norman Shawchuck, *A Guide to Prayer for Ministers and Other Servants* (Nashville: Upper Room, 1983), p. 320.

4. Wayne E. Oates, *The Christian Pastor,* 3rd ed., rev. (Philadelphia: Westminster Press, 1982), pp. 261–283, has an enlightening discussion concerning this "ministry of introduction."

5. Alan Jones, *Exploring Spiritual Direction* (New York: Seabury Press, 1982), p. 76.

For Further Reading

The following books may be helpful in pursuing an interest in transitions. While some have a specifically Christian orientation and others do not, all are nontechnical and highly readable.

Bridges, William. *Transitions: Making Sense of Life's Changes.* Reading, Mass.: Addison-Wesley Publishing Co., 1980.

De Mello, Anthony. *Sadhana: A Way to God, Christian Exercises in Eastern Form.* Garden City, N.Y.: Doubleday & Co., Image Books, 1984.

Jones, Alan. *Soul Making: The Desert Way of Spirituality.* San Francisco: Harper & Row, 1985.

O'Connor, Elizabeth. *Cry Pain, Cry Hope: Thresholds to Purpose.* Waco, Tex.: Word Books, 1987.

Viorst, Judith. *Necessary Losses.* New York: Fawcett Books, 1987.